Leadership from the Heart

Learning to Lead with Love and Skill

Leader's Guide

Abingdon Press

LEADERSHIP FROM THE HEART:
LEADER'S GUIDE

Scripture quotations in this publication, unless otherwise indicated, are taken from the *New Revised Standard Version of the Bible*, copyright 1989 by the Division of Christian Education of the National Council of the Churches of Christ in the United States of America. Used by permission. All rights reserved.

Those noted NIV are from the HOLY BIBLE, NEW INTERNATIONAL VERSION. Copyright © 1973, 1978, 1984 by International Bible Society. Used by permission of Zondervan Publishing House. All rights reserved.

Those noted NASB are from the New American Standard Bible, © The Lockman Foundation 1960, 1962, 1968, 1971, 1972, 1973, 1975, 1977. Used by permission.

Those noted NLT are from the *Holy Bible*, New Living Translation, copyright © 1996. Used by permission of Tyndale House Publishers, Inc. Wheaton, Illinois 60189. All rights reserved.

Those noted NKJV are from The New King James Version. Copyright © 1979, 1980, 1982, Thomas Nelson Inc., Publishers.

Those noted Msg. are taken from *The Message.* Copyright © Eugene H. Peterson, 1993, 1994, 1995. Used by permission of NavPress Publishing Group.

04 05 06 07 08 09 10 11 12 13—10 9 8 7 6 5 4 3 2 1

MANUFACTURED IN THE UNITED STATES OF AMERICA

Contents

INTRODUCTION

Welcome to *Leadership from the Heart*! This study is designed to educate and equip God's people for servant-leadership both within the local congregation and in the community and world. The material grew out of the experiences of the Leadership Development team at the United Methodist Church of the Resurrection (Resurrection) in Leawood, Kansas. From the beginning, we realized the pastors and staff of Resurrection could not possibly provide all the leadership needed by every ministry within our church, nor were they meant to. This identified for us the need to develop new and emerging lay leaders to provide day-to-day leadership. Many churches recognize this need and seek to address it by developing their laity for leadership. Leadership within the church, however, is not leadership as the secular world defines it; it is *servant-leadership*. Understanding what servant-leadership is, and how to live it out, is the focus of this study.

The study begins with an introduction of the concept of servant-leadership followed by a nine-session exploration of three major aspects of servant-leadership, which are outlined in this servant-leader covenant:

I. Internal or Self-Leadership

I will model Christian behavior:
I will submit my life to the guidance of the Holy Spirit and the Word of God.
I will discover, develop, and use my God-given spiritual gifts.

II. Organizational or Church Leadership

I will uphold the vision and mission of my church:
I will share my faith as I seek to fulfill the Great Commission.
I will serve with a passionate commitment for ministry.

III. Relational or Team Leadership

I will guide others as we strive to realize our potential in Christ:
I will invest in lives with my time, knowledge, energy, and love.
I will elevate others through prayer, thoughts, words, and deeds.

I will offer my life in service for the glory of God.

As we explore internal leadership, we will discuss developing a personal relationship with Christ, growing towards spiritual maturity, and exploring a spiritual gifts-based ministry. Under the heading of church leadership, we will examine the importance of sharing our faith, serving others, and working toward church renewal. Finally, we will delve into relational leadership as we discuss the concepts of team ministry, building healthy teams, and caring for individual team members.

We have been training and equipping lay leaders at Resurrection for several years using this servant-leader covenant and study material, and the results have been amazing. Participants have come to understand God's concept of leadership and God's plan for their lives. Each year we have learned from our experiences and have modified the material accordingly. As a result, the format we suggest in this resource is one that has proven successful—both in teaching the concepts and engaging the interest of the participants.

All Christians are called to know God with their head, love God and neighbor with their heart, and serve God with their hands. Likewise, as servant-leaders, we are expected to model head, heart, and hands faith in our lives. Therefore, each chapter in the *Participant Book* (included in this *Leader's Guide* for your convenience) contains three major sections:

Head—Taking in information through reading and reflecting

Heart—Considering how the things we've learned apply to our lives and relationships

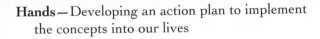

Hands—Developing an action plan to implement the concepts into our lives

Each week participants should read the appropriate chapter for the next session, respond to the reflection questions following the Biblical Foundation, and reflect on and respond to the questions in Taking It to Heart. In class, participants will watch a brief video presentation, discuss the Heart to Heart questions in small groups, and respond to the Action Plan section individually and, as instructed, with an accountability partner.

Instead of relying on lecture to *teach* the concepts, we suggest you act as *facilitator*, encouraging participants to learn from experience and one another. The curriculum utilizes a variety of teaching methods to appeal to different learning styles, ensuring that every participant engages in the experience. Active participation fosters *self-discovery*, which is the most effective way for adult learning to occur. When adults discover a truth for themselves through the process of reflection followed by discussion, they more readily personalize and internalize the information, leading to easier application and, ultimately, transformation. And that, after all, is the goal!

Each class session follows roughly the same format. Though the outlines in this *Leader's Guide* are designed for a ninety-minute class format, we have included suggestions for shortening the sessions to sixty minutes, as well as lengthening them to two hours. (We use a two-hour format at Resurrection, and we have found that it satisfies the participants' needs for learning and fellowship without seeming to burden them.)

The study is intended to utilize small groups, typically of six to eight people. We have found that small group members form a strong bond, encouraging one another as they learn and grow into servant-leadership. If you are using this curriculum in a group with less than twelve people, such as a Bible study group or Sunday school class, you still will want to separate into smaller groups for certain portions of each session. Using small groups increases the likelihood that all class members will participate, sharing their own experiences and insights.

Each small group should be assigned a small group "guide." The guide's role is to facilitate the small group discussions (not teach, but keep the discussion moving), to encourage and care for group members throughout the study, and to serve as time-keepers. You will want to recruit spiritually mature lay leaders—or, in the future, past participants of *Leadership from the Heart*—to serve as guides. If you are using this material with a group of less than twelve, you may serve as both class facilitator and small group guide.

The format for each session includes the following components, each of which serves an important purpose. We encourage you to use them all.

◆ *Opening Prayer and Welcome*: This serves as a "call to order," bringing the group together, gaining their attention, and introducing the topic for each session.

◆ *Opening Activity*: The opening activity each week is designed to help participants transition from their daily work, home, or school activities to the class and engage them so that they can focus on the topic at hand. The activities are done within small groups, using reflection or experiential learning (getting them to *do* something) to bring about an important discovery relating to the topic.

◆ *Video Presentation*: Each session has a short video presentation (10 minutes or less) taught by an expert on the session topic. The videos reinforce but do not duplicate the information in the chapters. Though all participants benefit, these video presentations are especially appealing to visual or auditory learners.

◆ *Full Group Discussions*: After each video presentation, there is a short discussion (5 minutes or so) which allows all class members to share general insights. This *Leader's Guide* contains questions to get you started. This full group discussion time helps the participants understand that their small group is part of a bigger whole, and that they can learn much about servant-leadership from the world and from one another.

◆ *Small Group Discussions*: This is the most important time during each session. During the small group time, participants develop deep bonds of friendship, sharing more personal insights as the program progresses. They will support and encourage one another as they come to understand that two Christians can have different insights and opinions on the same topic and still both be right, and that every person has something to offer in the discussion.

◆ *Accountability Partners*: The **Hands** portion of each session instructs the participants to develop an action plan for implementing the concepts they've learned into their ministries and their lives. Accountability partners encourage application of the concepts they are learning in class. Participants are more likely to follow through on their action plans when they know they will have to report on their progress the following week. This is critical if they are to achieve transformation. We strongly recommend you use "same gender" accountability partners. Not only does this protect against the risk of gossip or improper relationships; it also makes participants more likely to share honestly. In other words, it's simply more effective.

◆ *Closing Circle Prayer*: We have discovered that many people, even those currently serving in leadership positions, are uncomfortable praying aloud in a group. Circle prayers help participants become more comfortable praying aloud, which leaders are often called upon to do. With group members holding hands, have each person pray one sentence aloud, beginning with the small group guide. As each one prays, he or she squeezes the hand of the person on the right, signaling the next person's turn. When the circle comes to back to the small group guide, he or she closes the prayer. Guides should stress that the sentences don't have to be flowery or elaborate—just from the heart!

Before you begin *Leadership from the Heart*, here are some helpful tips to consider:

1. **Encourage early registration.** You'll need to know how many participants you'll have in order to recruit the appropriate number of small group guides, and you'll need time to assign each participant to a small group.

2. **Create a roster with addresses and phone numbers or e-mail addresses of all confirmed participants.** Make copies and distribute one to each participant during the orientation session (see below). Encourage group members, and especially accountability partners, to stay in contact during the week between sessions. Small group guides will need the roster in order to communicate with members of their groups, including following up with absentees.

3. **Hold an orientation session.** Use this opportunity to confirm the participant list and distribute the materials. Orientation is also a great time to give an overview of the program and to make certain that participants understand the commitment in terms of class time and the homework they'll need to do each week. Class participants will need to read the appropriate chapter and respond to the Biblical Foundation reflection questions and the Taking it to Heart questions prior to each session.

4. **Recruit your small group guides.** Provide each with a *Leader's Guide*, which will help them fulfill their role effectively. Review with them the responsibilities of a small group guide, and make certain they understand the role and feel they can fulfill it.

5. **Arrange for the meeting space and set-up.** We encourage you to have small groups sit around tables because this makes it easier for them to write and allows them to face one another, facilitating the discussion process. Review the equipment and materials you'll need for each session so that you won't be caught off guard by something you need but don't have.

6. **Assign participants to small groups.** Create a list of small groups. You can assign group numbers or group names (or allow the groups to pick their own names!). Have the list handy at the beginning of the first session so you can direct each participant to the appropriate table. You may want to create table signs, each with the group number or name and the group members' names, and place them at the tables, allowing group members to find their own tables if you're helping someone else and not available to assist them right away.

7. **Plan a graduation celebration.** Select a date ahead of time so participants can put it on their calendars. Have a time of worship with Holy Communion, if feasible, and an anointing service. This is a perfect way to "send forth" this new group of servant-leaders!

We pray that your church will be blessed by this material and by your work to build up the body of Christ by equipping God's people for servant-leadership. We believe that the Holy Spirit will be present with you, guiding you all the way. God bless you!

Tips for Small Group Guides

Your role as a small group guide carries four primary responsibilities: 1) to serve as a shepherd or resource, 2) to act as group facilitator, 3) to coach members toward spiritual growth, and 4) to be a role model. Below is a list of tips for successfully fulfilling each of these roles.

Serve as a Shepherd and Resource:

◆ Pray for your group members individually and collectively. Pray for their spiritual growth, and for them to recognize and respond to God's will for their lives as individuals. Pray that the group will bond, forming lasting relationships, and that they will be open and encouraging to one another.

◆ Be loving, full of grace, and encouraging. Be a representative of Christ's love for each member of your group.

◆ Follow up with a caring phone call or note when someone misses a session. If a group member experiences illness or has another need, suggest that the group provide support and care for their fellow group member during that period.

Act as Group Facilitator:

◆ Facilitate by asking questions. Don't "teach"; adults learn best by self-discovery. You are not expected to have all the answers; you're learning, too!

◆ Encourage everyone to participate. Each person's insights and experiences are valid. Draw out those people who tend to be reserved by asking for their insights. Control those who dominate the discussion by directing a question to another participant.

◆ Help the group use its time effectively. Keep the discussion on track, but be flexible if you sense the group members need extra time to understand a key point of learning.

Coach: Be a Partner in Growth

◆ Hold the members accountable for preparation and attendance. Challenge them to get the most out of each session.

◆ Urge participants to apply what they are learning in their lives. Remind them that the purpose of the program is not information input, but transformation.

◆ Encourage participants to listen for God's calling and purpose on their lives, and to serve in a way that utilizes their spiritual gifts.

Be a Role Model:

◆ Attend every session, arriving promptly and fully prepared. Set an example of the behavior expected from the group members.

◆ Establish trust by being authentic and open. Be willing to share your struggles and shortcomings. Group members will open up only after they see you being open and allowing yourself to be vulnerable.

◆ Be fully present, listening to each person as he or she speaks.

◆ Model servant-leadership for the group members.

SESSION 1

WHAT IS SERVANT-LEADERSHIP?

Learning to Lead from the Heart

Materials Needed:

◆ nametags
◆ pens or pencils
◆ TV and DVD player

For Opening Activity:
◆ paper or notecards for each small group

Room Set-up:

◆ Prior to beginning of class, all participants should be assigned to a group (under twelve participants: break into small groups of three to four; over twelve participants: break into small groups of six to eight).
◆ Arrange each group around a table, so members are facing one another, to facilitate discussion.
◆ Place TV and DVD player so that all can see (participants may need to turn their chairs around to view video).

Timing:

This outline is designed to cover a ninety-minute session. If you prefer to fit this into a sixty-minute format, we suggest reducing the Opening Activity to fifteen minutes and the Heart to Heart Small Group Discussion to fifteen minutes. If you prefer a two-hour format, include a fifteen-minute break after the Video Presentation Discussion, and add fifteen minutes to the Heart to Heart Small Group Discussion.

Opening Prayer and Welcome

(5 minutes)

Welcome members to *Leadership from the Heart*, Session 1. The purpose of this session is two-fold:

1. To get to know the other members of their groups.
2. To introduce the topic of servant-leadership and to gain an understanding of what servant-leadership is and why it's important to the Church.

Explain to participants that most sessions will follow the same general format as this evening's session. The curriculum is designed to be very interactive, with limited teaching from the front of the room. Each participant has been assigned to a small group, and these groups will remain together for the duration of the program. Each group has a "guide," who will serve as the group's facilitator. The guide is not a teacher but simply one who will start the discussions and keep them on track. Group members will get to know one another very well and will learn from one another. Participants will get out of the study what they put into it.

Opening Activity

(30 minutes)

This week's opening activity is longer and more involved than most subsequent weeks, and it is a great way to get started. It allows small group members to learn about one another and have fun at the same time, making it easier for them to bond. This is critical to helping individuals share openly with one another in the coming weeks. Do not skip this activity unless you have an existing, well-bonded group!

Divide participants into their pre-assigned small groups. For small groups of six to eight, have the groups break into triads or quads. Small groups of three to four can do the activity together as described. Group member A takes two minutes to talk about himself or

herself. Group member B takes notes on the facts as told, while group member C (and D) writes down things he or she infers from what person A says (*positive* things he or she *suspects* are true, i.e. "Based on what I heard, I believe Ann cares about the environment, so I think she recycles on a regular basis," or "Joe seems to be musically inclined, and I think he sings along *loudly* to music in his car"). Keep your inferences positive, but get creative and have fun with this! Group members then trade responsibilities and repeat the process.

After all group members have talked about themselves in the triads/quads, have the small groups come back together and take turns introducing each other to the whole small group, with one person stating the facts and another stating the inferences. Small groups of only three or four may rejoin the full group and take turns introducing each other to the entire class.

Video Presentation

Dan Entwistle (Approx. 10 minutes)

Play the video segment for Session 1.

Full Group Video Discussion

(5 minutes)

Facilitate a full group discussion based on the video presentation using the questions that follow. Don't be nervous if no one responds immediately. If there is a pause and you do not fill in the silence, someone eventually will speak up! After someone responds, ask for other comments. After one or two comments, go on to the next question, and so forth. Try to keep this initial discussion brief and to the point. Inform the participants that more in-depth discussion will follow in their small groups.

1. The speaker stated that many of us feel apprehensive about serving in a leadership role. In your opinion, why are we apprehensive?

2. The speaker mentioned several shifts in values and perspectives that occur as we grow into servant-leadership. How have you experienced these shifts or seen them in others?

3. What other insights did you glean from the video?

Bring the group back to this key point:
Servant-leadership is Christ's model for leadership. Servant-leadership is contrary to our human nature; living into it requires change in us.

Heart to Heart Small Group Discussions

(30 minutes)

Each small group guide should start the discussion by reminding group members that the discussion questions are not designed to have "right" or "wrong" answers. They are meant to encourage group members to share their own insights and experiences, as well as what they've learned, so that members of the group can learn from one another. Everyone has something to offer! The guide should encourage each person to participate and should keep any one individual from dominating the discussion. Refer to the Tips for Small Group Guides in this *Leader's Guide* (page 8) for pointers on group facilitation.

Begin by asking the group to summarize the video presentation. Groups should try to get that message into a few short sentences.

Ask group members which passage(s) from this week's Scripture reading spoke to them and why.

Continue the discussion using the Heart to Heart questions on page 18.

Hands Action Plan

(5 minutes)

Have each person choose a *same gender* accountability partner for the duration of the study (some groups may have to form accountability trios). This will provide some continuity in the accountability partners' discussions.

First, they spend one to two minutes responding individually to the questions in the Hands portion of the session on page 18; then they share their responses (their Action Plan) with their accountability partner(s). Next week they will report their progress to their accountability partner(s).

Closing Circle Prayer

(5 minutes)

Small group guides should bring the accountability partners of the small groups back together for joys and concerns and a closing prayer. Ask the participants to keep their comments brief, encouraging them to share detailed prayer requests outside of class time—either in person, on the phone, or via e-mail.

We encourage you to use a circle prayer format to close the small group time. The ability to lead a group in prayer is essential in Christian leadership, but many people are not comfortable praying aloud. Circle prayers are useful in helping people become comfortable praying in a group. Remind the participants that their words do not have to be elaborate— only from the heart!

Have members stand, if they are able, holding hands around the table. Ask each person to speak one sentence in prayer, with the small group guide opening and closing the prayer.

WHAT IS SERVANT-LEADERSHIP?
CHAPTER 1 Learning to Lead from the Heart

"And David shepherded them with integrity of heart…" (Psalm 78:72a)

 **HEAD**

Key Insights

◆ Christian servant-leadership is different from leadership in the secular or corporate world; it is leadership from the *heart*—leadership with a focus on…
- knowing and doing the will of God, following the example of Christ,
- appreciating others' worth and valuing their needs, and
- leading others toward a deeper walk with Christ.

◆ Servant-leadership is evident in an individual's character and behaviors.

◆ Although developing yourself as a Christian servant-leader involves intensive internal work, your efforts will lead you to know *intuitively* whom and what to follow, and when and where to lead.

Understanding the Concept

Servant-leadership manifests itself in three ways:

1) through submission to Christ (*a heart surrendered to Christ and his church*),
2) in service to others (*a heart that loves and serves its neighbor*), and
3) in response to the Holy Spirit (*a heart filled with the Holy Spirit and moved to respond obediently, as evidenced by one's character and behavior*).

Given this description, who could argue with becoming a servant-leader? The difficulty lies not in understanding servant-leadership, but in putting it into practice. It takes a "work of heart." It is a process and a journey—one taken by imperfect human beings who are capable of doing good but prone to wandering off the path.

This is not a journey you should undertake unless you are ready to grow up—to mature in your faith. Noted authors Ken Blanchard and Phil Hodges write, "The journey of life is to move from a self-serving heart to a serving heart. You finally become an adult when you realize that life is about what you give, rather than what you get" (*The Servant Leader: Transforming Your Heart, Head, Hands & Habits* [Nashville: J. Countryman, 2003], p.22). Jesus modeled what this means for us as He gave his very life in the service of others.

If you're thinking that becoming a servant-leader takes intentional effort and hard work, you're right. Lest you become discouraged, it is also a journey filled with great rewards. There is nothing more rewarding than investing your life in fulfilling God's purposes—for yourself and for others. The church reaps the benefits of servant-leadership as ministries become more effective and life in the body of Christ is enhanced. It is an awesome feeling to know you have invested your life in something of eternal value, and it's a privilege to watch God bring about eternal results.

Definitions of a Servant-leader

What exactly is a "servant-leader"? It seems to be a contradictory term. We will define each word separately:

Servant—a person hired to perform services for another; a person ardently devoted to another or to a cause or creed. (Note: Sometimes "servant" is used interchangeably in Scripture with the word "slave," which means a human being who is owned as property by another and is under his or her absolute control.)

Leader— a person who leads; a directing, commanding, or guiding head, as of a group or activity (Note: The word "leader" actually never appears in the New Testament. Jesus at times used "Master," which is translated from the Greek word *διδασκαλὄς*, meaning doctor, master, or teacher.)

A "servant-leader," then, is someone who both serves others (meets needs) and leads others (directs or guides). As Christian servant-leaders, we serve and lead as people wholly devoted to Jesus Christ. As our faith grows and deepens, our attitudes and perspectives become more and more Christ-like. This shift affects how we live and lead. We begin to care less about the power and prestige of leading, and more about serving others and serving God. For example, when we first joined the church, we may have been more interested in what the church could do to serve us. As we grow and mature, our focus shifts from meeting our own needs to serving others' needs.

In his book *Servant Leadership*, Robert K. Greenleaf says that a great leader is known first as a servant. This was true even of Jesus, who said of himself, "Even the Son of Man did not come to be served, but to serve" (Mark 10:45). Leadership develops only when followers place trust and confidence in someone they have known first as a servant. When a new leader comes into the picture—whether in the role of teacher, boss, or pastor—there is always a "getting-to-know-you" period in which those being led evaluate whether or not this person can be trusted not only to lead, but also to protect the best interests of those being led. When we know that a leader has our best interests at heart and truly cares about us, we open up to him or her and develop a personal relationship. This results in a willingness on our parts to follow, because trust has formed.

Consider your own church and its servant power potential. What might God accomplish through a body of believers yielded to his purpose and ready and willing to be in service to others? Think of the potential of inspired and empowered leaders, and of followers who are ready to be led.

Roles of a Servant-leader

The roles of a servant-leader and a follower go hand-in-hand. There are no leaders without followers and, conversely, no followers without leaders. At any given moment, you will find you are in the position of being one or the other. Both are necessary, and both are equally important roles. A leader sees what needs to be done

> "It is not enough for the priests and ministers of the future to be moral people, well trained, eager to help their fellow humans, and able to respond creatively to the burning issues of their times. All of that is very valuable and important, but it is not the heart of Christian leadership. The central question is—Are the leaders of the future truly men and women of God, people with an ardent desire to dwell in God's presence, to listen to God's voice, to look at God's beauty, to touch God's incarnate Word and to taste fully God's infinite goodness?"
>
> ~Henry Nouwen,
> *In the Name of Jesus*

and is willing to take the risk of helping others to move in that direction—providing vision and direction. A follower empowers the leader in this role by taking the risk of trusting his or her insight.

In addition to providing vision and direction, a servant-leader has the role of bringing about healing and wholeness by helping individuals to see and embrace God's plan or purpose for their lives. Think of the example of Jesus. As he traveled about, Jesus healed the sick and helped those to whom he ministered envision a brighter future in the kingdom of God. Servant-leaders concern themselves with the health and well-being of the individuals and the organizations they serve by nurturing spiritual growth, encouraging and enabling a sense of community, living as an example to those they lead by being vulnerable and committed, and by giving of themselves.

Are you comfortable in the role of leader? What about the role of follower? Which comes more naturally to you? You must be spiritually prepared for *both* roles by being open to the guidance of the Holy Spirit through the practice of spiritual disciplines, and by developing an awareness of our spiritual giftedness. This awareness is important because an individual may not have one of the leadership gifts yet may be in a situation where he or she is thrust into temporary leadership. On the other hand, an individual who does have leadership gifts may be in the follower role in certain settings or situations. We'll discuss these topics further in later chapters.

The Character of a Servant-leader

The character of a servant-leader is a reflection of the leader's personal relationship with God, just as Jesus' character was a reflection of his relationship with the Father. A true servant-leader desires and demonstrates character that continually is becoming more and more like the character of Christ— authentic, vulnerable, grace-filled, responsive, personally involved and engaged, accepting,

> ### "What you do as a leader will depend on who you are."
> —James A. Autry, *The Servant Leader*

trustworthy, loving, caring, spiritual, passionate, and patient, to name a few. Overall, these traits are associated more with *being* than with *doing*. Chief among them is *being authentic*.

Being authentic is simply knowing yourself and then being yourself. How do you "know yourself"? One way is through the practice of spiritual disciplines—meditating on the Word of God, praying, reading and studying the Bible, spending time in solitude, and living a simple life. We'll learn more about these disciplines later; for now, suffice it to say that being authentic is about being your true self in all circumstances.

Knowing our true selves is only possible through an ongoing process of introspection. Each of us has strengths and weaknesses, both in our behaviors and in our character. We need to reflect on these and strive to improve in those areas where we are far from Christ's model. As we continue doing this difficult, intentional, disciplined "work of heart," our character and behaviors will more closely mirror those of Jesus. Practically speaking, we will know we are becoming an authentic servant-leader when we demonstrate the same character traits and behaviors when we are alone and no one is watching as we do when we are teaching a class at church!

Becoming a Servant-leader

So, *how* do you become a servant-leader? As we've mentioned, it is a process and a journey that takes time and effort. There are, however, some practical "guidelines" that can help you along the way. Let's take a look at a "Servant-leader Covenant" that outlines some specific character and behavioral attributes in which all servant-leaders should seek to grow.

1. Serving as a Role Model

I will model Christian behavior:
I will submit my life to the guidance of the Holy Spirit and the Word of God.

I will discover, develop, and use my God-given spiritual gifts.

This section of the covenant refers to the servant-leader as a role model. Others will look to us, and at us, by virtue of our leadership positions. If we are to fulfill a guiding role in the church, we must be careful to be authentic in our personal relationship with Jesus Christ. This involves submitting ourselves to His lordship and allowing the Holy Spirit to lead and guide us in all circumstances. We do this as we open ourselves to His leading through prayer, Bible study, and the encouragement and accountability of Christian brothers and sisters.

We also model Christian behavior as the Holy Spirit empowers us for service through our God-given spiritual gifts. Spiritual gifts, by nature, benefit other members of the body of Christ, and, ultimately, their employment honors and glorifies God. Discovering, developing, and using our spiritual gifts demonstrates our faithfulness and obedience to God's calling on our lives. As servant-leaders, we also must affirm and encourage the gifts we see in other people.

Steve, a member of our church, was so impacted by our *Serving from the Heart* class that he wanted to be a part of that ministry which focused on spiritual gifts discovery. At the time, our team consisted of teachers who offered the class at various times, so Steve signed up to teach. One session of team teaching reinforced for him the importance of serving according to one's giftedness. Teaching was not for him! He still wanted strongly to be part of the ministry, so we created a new position for him that would allow him to use his exceptional administration gift. Five years later, Steve is still using his gifts in this ministry area, taking care of all the details and freeing the teachers to do what they need to do. As a result, Steve has experienced tremendous spiritual growth. When he first joined the gifts team, Steve was reluctant to pray out loud. Now he not only prays in groups, but he also is helping others in their spiritual growth by serving as a guide in a leadership development class.

2. Upholding the Church's Vision and Mission
I will uphold the vision and mission of (church name):
I will share my faith as I seek to fulfill the Great Commission.

I will serve with a passionate commitment for ministry.

Servant-leaders are challenged to embrace and embody the purpose, vision, mission, and values of their own church. These represent God's specific direction and purpose for a particular body in Christ's greater church. As the servant-leaders of a church embrace the church's vision, they serve as a catalyst for renewal not only within their respective churches, but also within the church at large. All servant-leaders should lead the way in sharing their faith and being "salt and light" outside the church, working together to transform individuals and the community.

In these ways and more, servant-leaders serve with passion—enthusiasm for God's purposes. There is no greater calling than knowing God and serving him with all we have and all we are. In Romans 12:1, the apostle Paul admonishes us to "offer [our] bodies as living sacrifices, holy and pleasing to God—this is [our] spiritual act of worship." We should joyfully give ourselves as living sacrifices for his service as we live out God's good and perfect plans for our lives.

Our church has a three-fold vision: transforming lives, transforming the community, and renewing the church at large. Local public schools have been in decline for years, seriously undermining the morale of school employees. Two years ago, our pastor gathered a list of all employees in the school system and asked each member to take one name, pray for that person, and then write the individual a note. The response was incredible; the people serving in the schools felt acknowledged and encouraged. One woman in our church felt strongly about carrying this even further, and she recruited members of our church to volunteer their time to serve as tutors and mentors for the students of these schools. What an impact that ministry is having in the lives of the individuals they are helping, as well as in the future of our community.

3. Guiding Others
I will guide others as we strive to realize our potential in Christ:
I will invest in lives with my time, knowledge, energy, and love.

I will elevate others through prayer, thoughts, words, and deeds.

The mark of a true servant is to appreciate the worth of others and place value on serving their needs. Servant-leaders pour themselves into the lives of other people. They do this by investing their time; knowledge; resources; physical, spiritual, and emotional energy; and unconditional love in others' lives. Some of the tools used to accomplish this are intercessory prayer, God-honoring thoughts, encouraging words, and tangible actions.

Sam is the audio ministry director at our church. Young people are often attracted to serving in his ministry area. One teenage volunteer got into some trouble and was sent to a juvenile detention center. Instead of writing this boy off, Sam prayed for him, visited the young man repeatedly, and encouraged him to turn his life around. Sam gave of himself physically and emotionally as he unselfishly tried to meet the needs of someone else.

Another example of investing in the lives of others might be to encourage their growth by providing ongoing training, both inside and outside the church. For instance, if your church or another is having a conference relating to your ministry area, try to provide opportunities to attend—either as individuals, or as a group.

4. Serving Others

I offer my life in service for the glory of God.

In 1 Peter 4:11 we read, "Whoever speaks must do so as one speaking the very words of God; whoever serves must do so with the strength that God supplies, so that God may be glorified in all things through Jesus Christ. To him belong the glory and the power forever and ever. Amen." We are to use all our gifts, talents, and abilities to serve others, not just to benefit ourselves.

Sometimes we can get caught up in the attention we receive when we exercise our gifts, or are tempted to exercise them, for our own purposes. For example, someone may be tempted to serve in order to make business contacts. That is not the motive of a servant-leader. We need to remember that we serve for God's glory, not our own. When we are faithful to do this, others will see Jesus' love shine through us and give praise to God for the results.

> "Jesus…is only a prayer away as your leadership guide and inspiration. You're not called to lead by yourself."
>
> —**Ken Blanchard,** *The Servant Leader*

Looking Ahead

Future chapters will provide you with opportunities for in-depth study of each section of the servant-leader covenant. This is just the beginning of your journey—the first step toward your development as a servant-leader. Each week will build on the foundation of the prior weeks' key insights. We also will work on the external aspects of servant-leadership so that you are developing the skills necessary to help you lead. Through it all, the Holy Spirit will be available to guide and encourage you. Real help is only a prayer away!

Biblical Foundation

As you review each Scripture passage, underline or circle key words or phrases. Think about the implications of each passage for your life, noting your insights in the space provided. Answer the questions that follow.

Then the mother of the sons of Zebedee came to Jesus with her sons, and kneeling before him, she asked a favor of him. And he said to her, "What do you want?" She said to him, "Declare that these two sons of mine may sit, one at your right hand and one at your left, in your kingdom." But Jesus answered, "You do not know what you are asking. Are you able to drink the cup that I am about to drink?" They said to him, "We are able." He said to them, "You will indeed drink my cup, but to sit at my right and at my left, this is not mine to grant, but it is for those for whom it has been prepared by my Father." When the ten heard it, they were angry with the two brothers. But Jesus called them to him and said, "You know that the rulers of the Gentiles lord it over them, and their great ones are tyrants over them. It will not be so among you; but whoever wishes to be great among you must be your servant, and whoever wishes to be first among you must be your slave; just as the Son of Man came not to be served, but to serve, and to give His life a ransom for many." (Matthew 20:20-28)

(For further study, read this story as told in Mark 10:35-45.)

Now before the festival of the Passover, Jesus knew that his hour had come to depart from this world and go to the Father. Having loved his own who were in the world, he loved them to the end. The devil had already put it into the heart of Judas son of Simon Iscariot to betray him. And during supper Jesus, knowing that the Father had given all things into his hands, and that he had come from God, and was going to God, got up form the table, took off his outer robe, and tied a towel around himself. Then he poured water into a basin and began to wash the disciples' feet and to wipe them with the towel that was tied around him. He came to Simon Peter, who said to him, "Lord, are you going to wash my feet?" Jesus answered, "You do not know now what I am doing, but later you will understand." Peter said to him, "You will never wash my feet." Jesus answered, "Unless I wash you, you have no share with me." Simon Peter said to him, "Lord, not my feet only but also my hands and my head!" Jesus said to him, "One who has bathed does not need to wash, except for the feet, but is entirely clean. And you are clean, though not all of you." For he knew who was to betray him; for this reason he said, "Not all of you are clean." After he had washed their feet, had put on his robe, and had returned to the table, he said to them, "Do you know what I have done to you? You call me Teacher and Lord – and you are right, for that is what I am. So if I, your Lord and Teacher, have washed your feet, you also ought to wash one another's feet. For I have set you an example, that you also should do as I have done to you. Very truly, I tell you, servants are not greater than their

master, nor are messengers greater than the one who sent them. If you know these things, you are blessed if you do them." (John 13:1-17)

"The greatest among you will be your servant. All who exalt themselves will be humbled, and all who humble themselves will be exalted." (Matthew 23:11-12)

Reflection Questions

1. After reflecting on these Bible passages, what would you say is Jesus' definition of leadership?

2. How would the disciples' view of leadership contrast with your answer to question 1?

3. What transpired immediately before Jesus got up from the supper? What did Jesus fully realize at this point in the story? In light of that, do the actions that follow make sense? Why or why not?

4. What method(s) of teaching did Jesus' employ to get His point across?

5. What was Jesus' motivation for teaching these truths? Answer from the perspective of the disciples and from your perspective.

6. From where does greatness come? What kind of greatness do you seek?

HEART

Taking It to Heart

1. Think of leaders who have impacted or influenced you. Do any of them fit the description of servant-leader? What was it about their leadership that you would like to emulate? What characteristics and behaviors would you not want to emulate?

2. Write your own definition of servant-leadership.

3. Examine your leadership history. Write or draw your own leadership timeline. Include leadership roles both inside and outside of the church.

4. As you reflect upon your timeline, what kind of a leader have you been at various stages of your life?

5. What qualities are important in a servant-leader in the church?

6. Why is it so important for Christian leaders to have a solid spiritual foundation for their lives and leadership?

Heart to Heart

1. As a group, develop a two- to three-sentence summary of the video presentation.

2. Discuss the Scripture passages from this week's reading. How would you define servant-leadership, according to Scripture? How does servant-leadership differ from leadership in the secular world?

3. In your group, share an example from your own experience when someone provided servant-leadership. Provide specific characteristics and/or behaviors.

4. How does the concept of servant-leadership translate into our daily lives?

HANDS

Action Plan

1. Which of the qualities important to leadership in the church do you need to work on? How will you begin to put that into action in the next week (your "action plan")?

2. Select a same-gender accountability partner (or partners) from your group. Take turns briefly sharing your action plan. Next week you'll discuss your progress.

3. The quality of your leadership is proportional to the level of your spiritual preparedness for leadership. Spend time every day this week in prayer and Bible study as you prepare your heart for servant-leadership.

DRAWING NEAR TO GOD

Developing a Personal Relationship with Christ Through the Spiritual Disciplines

SESSION 2

Materials Needed:

◆ nametags
◆ pens or pencils
◆ TV and DVD player

For opening activity:
◆ fresh tomatoes
◆ toy cars
◆ blank sheets of paper

Room Set-up:

◆ Arrange pre-assigned small groups around tables so that members are facing one another.
◆ Place TV and DVD player so that all can see (participants may need to turn their chairs around to view video).

Timing:

This outline is designed to cover a ninety-minute session. If you prefer to fit this into a sixty-minute format, we suggest deleting the Opening Activity and reducing the Heart to Heart Small Group Discussion to thirty minutes and the Hands Action Plan to ten minutes. If you prefer a two-hour format, include a fifteen-minute break after the Video Presentation Discussion, and add fifteen minutes to the Heart to Heart Small Group Discussion.

Opening Prayer and Welcome

(5 minutes)

Welcome participants to *Leadership from the Heart*, Session 2. The purpose of this session is to discover the importance of practicing the spiritual disciplines in developing an intimate relationship with God.

Opening Activity

(10 minutes)

Do not share the purpose of this activity with participants until after the activity is completed. Doing so will undermine the process of self-discovery, which is important for adult learning.

The purpose of this activity is to help participants realize that developing a relationship with Christ requires intentional and regular nurturing.

Give half of the small groups a fresh tomato, and the other half a toy car. Give all the groups a blank sheet of paper. Have the groups who have been given a fresh tomato write from start to finish the process for growing world-class, prize-winning tomatoes; instruct the groups who have been given a toy car to write from start to finish the process for changing a flat tire. Allow three minutes for them to complete the assignment.

Bring the full group back together. Ask the groups who were assigned the "flat tire" to call out the process they have recorded. Do the same with the "tomato" groups. Allow three minutes for this.

Use the following questions to generate a short discussion (allow four minutes for this):

How are these processes different?
In what ways is developing a relationship with Christ more like growing world-class tomatoes than changing a flat tire?
How does that relate to our topic of spiritual disciplines?

Video Presentation

Laurie Barnes (Approx. 12 minutes)

Play the video segment for Session 2.

Full Group Video Discussion

(5 minutes)

Facilitate a full group discussion based on the video presentation using the questions that follow. Don't be nervous if no one responds immediately. If there is a pause and you do not fill in the silence, someone eventually will speak up! After someone responds, ask for other comments. After one or two comments, go on to the next question, and so forth. Try to keep this initial discussion brief and to the point. Inform the participants that more in-depth discussion will follow in their small groups.

1. A prevailing topic in the video presentation was "holiness." The speaker said that Christians are called to pursue holiness—that holiness is the goal of Christian life. What does that mean to you?
2. The speaker related practicing the spiritual disciplines to training for sports or practicing a musical instrument. In what ways is that true?
3. What other insights did you glean from the video?

Bring the group back to this key point:
Spiritual disciplines are our means of developing a personal relationship with Christ, and are one of his means of changing us. We must be intentional about practicing the disciplines if we are to become more Christ-like.

Heart to Heart Small Group Discussions

(40 minutes)

Each small group guide should start the discussion by reminding group members that the discussion questions are not designed to have "right" or "wrong" answers. They are meant to encourage group members to share their own insights and experiences, as well as what they've learned, so that members of the group can learn from one another. Everyone has something to offer! The guide should encourage each person to participate, and should keep any one individual from dominating the discussion. Refer to the Tips for Small Group Guides in this *Leader's Guide* (page 8) for pointers on group facilitation.

Begin by asking the group to summarize the video presentation. Groups should try to get that message into a few short sentences.

Ask group members which passage(s) from this week's Scripture spoke to them and why.

Continue the discussion using the Heart to Heart questions on page 34.

Hands Action Plan

(15 minutes)

Small group guides should direct group members to get with their accountability partner(s) and proceed with the Hands portion of the session on page 34.

First, they each take one minute reporting their progress on last week's action plan. What did and did not happen as they had hoped?

Next, they take six to eight minutes developing their action plans for this week.

Finally, each one shares his or her action plan for the upcoming week.

Closing Circle Prayer

(5 minutes)

Small group guides should bring the accountability partners of the small groups back together for joys and concerns and a closing prayer. Ask the participants to keep their comments brief, encouraging them to share detailed prayer requests outside of class time— either in person, on the phone, or via e-mail.

We encourage you to use a circle prayer format to close the small group time. The ability to lead a group in prayer is essential in Christian leadership, but many people are not comfortable praying aloud. Circle prayers are useful in helping people become comfortable praying in a group. Remind the participants that their words do not have to be elaborate—just from the heart!

Have members stand, if they are able, holding hands around the table. Ask each person to speak one sentence in prayer, with the small group guide opening and closing the prayer.

DRAWING NEAR TO GOD
Developing a Personal Relationship with Christ through the Spiritual Disciplines

"Draw near to God, and he will draw near to you." (James 4:8)

CHAPTER 2

 HEAD

Key Insights

◆ The state of our spiritual health is a direct result of our relationship with God through Jesus Christ.

◆ We can strengthen that relationship through the practice of spiritual disciplines.

Understanding the Concept

What makes someone a Christian? Is it simply belief in Christ? James tells us that "Even the demons believe—and shudder" (2:19). There must be more to being a Christian than mere belief. Many people profess to be Christians because they attend church regularly. That's like saying swimming in the ocean makes someone a fish! There must be more to being a Christian than going to church. The truth is that Christianity is a relational faith. We are called into relationship with God through Jesus Christ.

When Christ breathed his last breath, the curtain in the temple separating the Holy Place from the Holy of Holies was ripped in two (Matthew 27:51). This symbolized the fact that Christ's death and subsequent resurrection gave us direct access to God through him. Christ himself became our high priest and our intercessor (Hebrews 4:14-16; 5:8-10; 7:25-27). The door opened for us to be in a personal relationship with the Creator of the universe.

Like any relationship, a deep relationship with God through Christ doesn't just happen; it must be developed and nurtured. Unfortunately, many Christians are never taught *how* to do this. The way to develop this relationship is through the practice of spiritual disciplines.

What Are Spiritual Disciplines?

Spiritual disciplines are things we do as a means of communicating with, learning from, or giving service to God. Although the number and name of the disciplines vary from author to author, there are several that are universally mentioned: 1) prayer, 2) study, 3) solitude and simplicity, 4) worship, 5) service, 6) fasting, and 7) confession. Regular practice of these disciplines moves us along the journey of faith from our initial state of new believers into mature, deeply committed Christians. John Wesley, founder of Methodism, called the spiritual disciplines "works of piety," or works of holiness. Becoming holy, or Christ-like, in character is a process that lasts our entire lifetimes.

Unfortunately, many people don't make practicing spiritual disciplines a priority because the term "discipline" sounds difficult, unpleasant, or perhaps even painful. In truth, making the spiritual disciplines a part of your life *does* require discipline, but this simply means it takes attention and practice. Practicing spiritual disciplines is not meant to be drudgery. The goal of the disciplines is to bring us into intimacy with God, who provides comfort, guidance, and joy as he molds us into the people he wants us to be.

Another misconception is that spiritual disciplines are only for the fanatically religious, spiritual giants, or clergy. Actually, they are for *all* of us. No special skill or knowledge is required. The only requirement is a desire to know God. Let's take a look at each one of the disciplines and consider how it can help us to know God better.

Exploring the Disciplines

1. Prayer

Do not worry about anything, but in everything by prayer and supplication with thanksgiving let your requests be made known to God. (Philippians 4:6)

How to Pray

Talking to God

Unfortunately, we tend to hide our deepest emotions when we pray—coming to God "on our best behavior," politely saying the words we think we should, and wearing masks over our broken hearts. The reality is that God already knows what we are thinking and feeling. God gives us the freedom either to share those thoughts and feelings with him, or not to share them. However, it is only by sharing our thoughts and feelings honestly with God that our relationship with him begins to grow, starting us on the journey toward spiritual maturity. When we tell God that we are angry at someone, or are disappointed by being passed over for a promotion at work, or are longing for recognition for something we have done, God can help us put those things in perspective or guide us back to his will. We can trust God not to hold our thoughts and feelings against us, but to lead us lovingly to the truth. As we pray authentically, we often find that our perspective was skewed toward the things of the world and away from God. Then, as the Holy Spirit leads us to the truth, we begin to see God, ourselves, and our thoughts and feelings honestly and with greater clarity. As a result, we are led to confession and repentance; and though our situation may not change, we are restored to a right relationship with God and find a renewed sense of joy and peace.

Just as there are no "right" words to say—and nothing we should *not* share with God—so also there is no single "right" way to pray. In fact, there are as many different ways to pray as there are people! The Bible includes examples of people praying in a variety of positions—while standing, kneeling, sitting, and lying prostrate on the ground—never suggesting one is better than the other. The same is true of places to pray. Throughout Scripture, we find people praying in the temple, in bed, in the fields, on a hillside, on the seashore, and in the privacy of a room. Our individual personalities make our styles of praying individual, too. Find a position and place that feels comfortable for you and enhances your attentiveness toward God.

If you need or want some guidance, there are a number of helpful prayer formats or models, though none is required, and no one format is better than any other. In fact, using different methods of prayer from time to time can enrich your prayer life. Still, you may find that certain formats are more appealing or comfortable to you than others. For example, you might like to use a simple acrostic, such as ACTS, to facilitate your personal prayers:

> **A**doration
> **C**onfession
> **T**hanksgiving
> **S**upplication

Begin with adoration, worshiping the Lord for who he is. Then, enter into confession, admitting your mistakes and failings to God. Step three is Thanksgiving, when you show appreciation for what God has done in your life—including forgiving the sins you have just confessed. Finally, close with supplication, which is expressing your requests for others and yourself.

Jesus himself gave us a simple format for prayer, which we call the Lord's Prayer:

Our Father, who art in heaven, hallowed be thy name. (Worship)
Thy kingdom come, thy will be done, on earth as

> **"The Disciplines allow us to place ourselves before God so that he can transform us."**
>
> – Richard Foster, *Celebration of Discipline*

it is in heaven. (Surrender)

Give us this day, our daily bread. (Supplication)

Forgive us our trespasses, as we forgive those who trespass against us. (Confession)

Lead us not into temptation, but deliver us from evil. (Guidance)

For thine is the kingdom, and the power, and the glory, forever and ever. (Worship)

The Lord's Prayer is often recited during worship services as a corporate prayer, but there are a number of ways to incorporate it into your personal prayer life. You might follow its format while supplying your own words. Open by praising God. Then, offer your life in surrender to his will, make requests for the needs of others as well as your own needs, confess your sins, and ask for guidance. Finally, close by praising him again.

Another way to use the Lord's Prayer—as well as other passages in the Bible—as a guide for prayer is called "praying the Scriptures." In this type of prayer, you read one line of Scripture at a time and then personalize the line by restating it in a way that relates to your life. Using this prayer format with the Lord's Prayer might go something like this:

Our Father, who art in heaven, hallowed be thy name.
> *Almighty God, Creator of heaven and earth, I praise your name.*

Thy kingdom come, thy will be done, on earth as it is in heaven.
> *Abba, I struggle with wanting to be in control. Today, I desire to do your will, as your angels in heaven do.*

Give us this day our daily bread.
> *Lord, you know what I need better than I do; and I trust in you to provide.*

Forgive us our trespasses, as we forgive those who trespass against us.
> *Father, forgive me for yelling at my daughter last night. Teach me to respond with compassion, instead of reacting in anger.*

Lead us not into temptation, but deliver us from evil.
> *Implant your word in my heart, Lord, that I might resist worldliness and follow you.*

For thine is the kingdom, and the power, and the glory forever. Amen.
> *You are my Lord, and I will worship you forever. Amen.*

There is a wide variety of other prayer formats. Check with your local Christian bookstore or public library to find a selection of books on prayer. It is important to remember, however, that prayer formats are meant to be an aid to praying, not a mindless routine; and they never should completely replace simple, personal prayers.

Listening to God

As important as it is to talk to God, it is critical that we also spend time in prayer listening to God. Sometimes we recite a laundry list of things we want to say to God and consider ourselves done with prayer. We are missing so much when we do not stop to listen for God to speak to us. Though it's not always easy—our minds tend to wander, or we find ourselves drifting off to sleep if we're tired—listening is a vital part of prayer.

You might pause after appropriate sections of prayer, asking God to speak to you; or perhaps at the end of your prayer you might invite God to respond in some way. You may feel God's response internally, in your own thoughts or feelings, or you may receive his response at a later time through another avenue. God communicates to us in a number of ways: through other people's words or actions, nature, Scripture and other writings, the arts, and many others.

One thing to keep in mind is that our expectations for God's response can often be unrealistic. We look for immediate answers, or we expect God to suspend the laws of nature in order to give us what we want, or sometimes we simply expect God to grant each and every request we make. Scripture tells us we can "approach the throne of grace with boldness" (Hebrews 4:16) because God does listen and respond to our prayers and petitions, but nowhere in the Bible does it tell us that God will grant every request in our timing and in the manner we wish. God knows what we really need, and sometimes it is not what we ask for. He may not produce a miracle to preserve the life of someone we love, but he will be there to provide comfort and strength to get us through the difficult time. We may not get the promotion we pray for, but we may find less stress and more joy when we do not get it. The amazing thing is that God listens and responds. That, in itself, is something to give thanks for.

When to Pray

One thing is certain: The only way to learn to pray is to "just do it." To some, it may seem awkward at first, but it will become more comfortable as it becomes a habit. One of the best ways to make prayer feel more natural is to get in the habit of having silent conversations with God throughout the day as you are going about your everyday routines. For example, if you are facing a difficult conversation with a friend, you might pray in your heart for God to give you the words to say. Or, when you drop off a child at school or let your sixteen-year-old borrow the car, you might whisper under your breath, "Oh, Lord, keep him/her safe." Some call these inner conversations "arrow prayers." Others call them "breath prayers." Brother Lawrence, a seventeenth century monk, called this "practicing the presence of God." Perhaps this is what the apostle Paul meant when he encouraged us to "pray without ceasing" (1 Thessalonians 5:17).

In addition to this kind of continual conversation with God, it is important to set aside a regular time when you can pray privately without interruptions. It could be early in the morning, late at night, at lunchtime, in the car, or whatever works for you on a consistent basis. If you can't imagine finding time to do this every day, start by selecting two or three days a week to have a dedicated prayer time. Then, on the other days of the week, make an effort to be in a "praying frame of mind," shooting "arrow" or "breath prayers" to God throughout the day, with the goal of working up to a habit of daily prayer. Many people wonder how long they should spend in prayer every day. It is a very individual decision influenced by your situation in life, your personality, and other factors. Many people find just ten to fifteen minutes of dedicated prayer time a day to be fulfilling and effective. Find what works for you on a consistent basis, and do not compare yourself to

others. God knows you, loves you, and wants to hear from you.

2. Study

Do not be conformed to this world, but be transformed by the renewing of your minds, so that you may discern what is the will of God—what is good and acceptable and perfect. (Romans 12:2)

Why do we need to study the Bible? Isn't going to church and hearing a sermon enough "Bible teaching" for one week? The truth is, no. As Romans 12:2 indicates, we must "renew our minds" if we are to avoid being conformed to this world; and the only thing that can renew our minds is God's Word. When we renew our minds by reading the Scriptures, God's will is revealed to us; and through the guidance of the Holy Spirit, we are transformed.

The Bible is not only a history of the Jews and the early Christian church; it is a revelation from God—a handbook, so to speak, for how he wants us to relate to him and to one another. Jesus put it this way: "If you continue in my word, you are truly my disciples; and you will know the truth, and the truth will make you free" (John 8:31-32). The discipline of study is more than reading the Bible; it also involves meditating on what we've read—thinking about what it means and how it might be applied to our lives. The real goal of Bible study is not accumulating information, but achieving transformation. In other words, studying the Bible prepares us to live the Christian life.

So, how should we study the Bible? As with prayer, there are a number of ways to practice the discipline of study, and all of them are acceptable. The key is finding the method that works for you, so that you can practice it consistently. Some people get up early every morning to read Scripture and pray. Others do it in the evening before bed. Some study alone; others study with a spouse or in a group. Still others "read" and meditate on Scripture by listening to audio Bibles in the car during their daily commute.

If you prefer to study alone, you might find it helpful to use a devotional book. There are a variety of formats, approaches, and topics for virtually every style and preference. One common format includes a Scripture passage, a reflection or story that explains or illustrates the passage, and questions for reflection.

Another option is using a daily or weekly devotional magazine. Or, you might prefer to use a particular Bible study guide or Bible reading plan (there are several one-year Bibles that take you through the entire Bible in a year's time). Some pastors prepare a study guide to complement their sermons each week, including study helps such as selected Scripture passages, comments, and questions to consider.

Perhaps you need the accountability that comes from involvement in a Bible study group. In most groups, there are Scripture reading assignments for the week, which are discussed later in the group setting. Talking about what you're studying with others helps with both understanding and application.

Whether you study alone or with a group, you will learn more from the Scripture if you ask questions of the passages you are reading or hearing each day. For example, you might ask yourself these three questions:

1. What does this tell me about God?
2. What does this tell me about humans?
3. What does this tell me about God's relationship with humans?

Or, you might use the inductive Bible study method, which involves asking these questions:

Inductive Method
1) What does it say?
2) What does it mean?
3) How does it apply to my life?

Remember, the goal of Bible study is not only to *know* what it says, but also to be *transformed* by what it says.

Pay particular attention to those passages that seem to "speak" to you, those that are particularly applicable to your current circumstances or state of mind. Highlight them in your Bible, write them down in a journal, or write them on a sticky note and put it on your mirror. Begin to memorize these passages, and they will come to mind when you need

encouragement or comfort, or when you seek to comfort or strengthen another. (By the way, don't be afraid to write in your Bible. This will help you find key passages and remember what you've read and learned. Special dry highlighters that won't bleed through the pages are available at most Christian bookstores.)

There are numerous translations of the Bible that are true to the original manuscripts yet are written in a way that makes studying God's word accessible. In fact, they are even available in a variety of formats: audio CD's or tapes, electronic versions for computer or pocket PC, as well as the traditional written word. You may find it helpful to incorporate a variety of Bible translations in your study. Sometimes reading a passage in several translations brings a deeper understanding or appreciation of its meaning, because each translation may have slightly different wording or phrasing. You might want to select one translation you particularly like as your primary Bible, and have others on hand to supplement your study as needed or desired.

There are also several study tools to enhance your study of Scripture. For instance, there are Bible dictionaries which explain terms and concepts, and there are Bible commentaries which provide background information about the historical period, adding depth and interest to your study, as well as explanations and interpretations to help clarify the meaning of difficult to understand passages. One word of caution: As you get into Bible study, you will encounter different and contradictory interpretations of Scripture. Keep in mind that every one of the interpretations you read is a theory or opinion about Scripture written from the author's specific perspective and influenced by his or her church background, training, and life situation. Comparing several interpretations will help you gain some perspective, but do not forget to compare them with what *you* believe the passage means. Most important, consider whether the interpretation is in line with Scriptural teaching in general.

Though most of the Bible was written well over two thousand years ago, it is still relevant to our lives today. That is the beauty of God's word! It is not just a history book; it is our handbook for living.

Studying Scripture deepens our faith, enriches our understanding of God, and enables us to live out our faith in the world. We simply cannot be faithful followers of Christ without practicing the discipline of study.

3. Solitude and Simplicity

When Jesus realized that they were about to come and take him by force to make him king, he withdrew again to the mountain by himself. (John 6:15)

Solitude

We all need an occasional "attitude adjustment." We get caught up in the things of the world—material possessions, status, control, power, and so on—and forget what life is really about: relationships with God and other people. Jesus himself faced temptation, not only in the desert, but also when the people, awed by his teachings and miracles, sought to make him king. He retreated to remove himself from the situation and keep himself focused on the right things.

Most of our schedules are so jam-packed that it seems impossible to find time for solitude—but we must! We need times of solitude to orient ourselves toward God's standards. Without this time of reorientation, we are too easily influenced by the world's values. Solitude enables us to see the negative influences tempting us to conform to the world's values. It gives us an opportunity to hear the "still small voice" of God, bringing us back in line with his will and guiding us in our daily lives.

In *Celebration of Discipline*, Richard Foster recommends we take daily "little solitudes" as well as quarterly "extended solitudes" ([San Francisco: Harper Collins Publishers, 1998], pp. 105, 107). Little solitudes are those numerous moments we might have to ourselves each day—before everyone else wakes up, after they've gone to sleep, or as we take a bath or drive to work. Many of us spend our days going from one task to another, never pausing in between, finally dropping into bed at night tired, frazzled, and empty. In fact, we have so much to do and so many people depending on us that we feel guilty taking time for solitude! We fail to consider how a brief moment of solitude might help us cope

with and respond to life's demands in a more joyful, peaceful way. How would your day be different if you paused to watch the sunrise as you drank your coffee before the kids wake up, or if you turned off the radio during your commute to work, allowing the quiet to calm you? Would it be so bad to spend half an hour during the week letting your mind wander peacefully as you work on a favorite hobby? For the extended solitudes, Foster suggests we set aside three to four hours for contemplating our life direction and goals. You might begin with prayer, asking God to use this time to guide and renew you. Spend some time studying Scripture, and reflect on its meaning for your life. Take time for you—go for a walk in nature, take a nap, work on a quiet hobby. Follow this time with prayer, seeking God's guidance and focusing on his will. Invite God to adjust your thinking, your priorities, and your life. As your solitude comes to a close, reflect on the time you've spent, thanking God for his guidance and for his renewing presence.

Simplicity

Simplicity, like solitude, may seem easier said than done. Our culture encourages us not to live simple lives but, instead, to seek wealth and prestige. Living a simple life does not mean giving away all of your possessions. It refers more to an inner attitude than specific actions, though it does lead to an outward expression of this inner attitude. Here are a few suggestions for leading a simple life paraphrased from Richard Foster's *Celebration of Discipline*:

◆ Buy things because you need them, not to impress others.
◆ Learn to enjoy things for free: borrow instead of buying, or spend time in nature.
◆ Become more giving; give things away to other people who need them.
◆ Be straightforward in your speech.
◆ Don't buy or participate in anything that leads to the oppression of others.
◆ Reject things that distract you from seeking God first.

(Adapted from *Celebration of Discipline*, Richard Foster [San Francisco: Harper Collins Publishers, 1998], p. 91-95.)

Seeking *first* the kingdom of God is the point of solitude and simplicity. These disciplines serve to keep our hearts and minds focused on God, making our relationship with Him the most important thing in our lives.

4. Worship

"But the hour is coming, and is now here, when the true worshipers will worship the Father in spirit and truth; for the Father seeks such as these to worship him. God is Spirit, and those who worship him must worship in spirit and truth." (John 4:23-24)

The discipline of worship involves much more than attending a worship service each week, although this is an important aspect of worship. Jesus said that the most important commandment was to "love the Lord your God with all your heart, and with all your soul, and with all your mind, and with all your strength" (Mark 12:30). This is where true worship begins—when we pour our whole being into worshiping God.

How do we worship with our whole being? It begins with an attitude of expectancy—expecting to see and experience God at work in our lives and the lives of others each and every day, wherever we may be. Simply put, worshipping with our whole being is keeping our focus on God at all times. Let's consider what this means for corporate worship, as well as for individual worship in our everyday lives.

Corporate Worship

Both the Israelites of the Old Testament and the disciples of the early church entered worship with an expectation that God would speak to them, either directly or indirectly through the words of the preacher, the words of the songs, or the presence of the Holy Spirit. Whether you prefer a more liturgical style of worship with responsive readings, or a traditional style with full choir, or a contemporary style with a band, be "fully present" during your weekly worship. Before the weekly worship service you attend, take time to prepare your heart by praising God in advance for the opportunity to worship him. Arrive a few minutes early and pray for the preacher, the music leaders, and others involved in worship, asking God to speak through them. Then pray that the hearts and minds of all those attending the service, including yours, will be open to receive whatever God wants each of you to hear or learn.

Pay attention to the rituals of your particular worship service. In some congregations, the service begins with the cross and lights for the altar candles being carried down the aisle. These represent the presence of Christ and the Holy Spirit coming into the room. Say a "breath prayer" of thanks for their presence in the midst of the gathering. In other congregations, worship includes liturgical responsive readings, which are traditional readings that have, in some cases, been repeated in worship services for hundreds of years, linking the participants to a historical community of faith. The Eucharist, also known as Holy Communion or the Lord's Supper, is another ritual of worship, by which we profess Jesus as Lord as individuals and as a community, just as the early church did so long ago.

When songs are sung, close your eyes if you like and really "hear" the words of the songs. Sing them with your heart, not just your mouth. Keep in mind that the Bible says we should sing a "joyful" song to the Lord and praise Him with "shouts of joy." Nowhere does it say we should sing "only if we have a good voice." So sing, and worship your God!

Worship is much more than music. Focus on God during *every* aspect of worship: prayer, the sermon or message, and even the offering time. In order to be "fully present" during corporate prayer, think about the words being said. As the pastor or other worship leader prays, you might restate and personalize his or her words silently as you listen. If your congregation recites the Lord's Prayer together, do not simply say the words but think about what they mean as you say them. Make it a personal prayer. During the sermon—or the drama/video message if your church uses these media—consider how the teaching applies to your life. What message does God have for you? As you place your tithe or offering into the plate, say an "arrow prayer," thanking God for the gifts and blessings he has provided. Throughout the service, guard against distractions and keep your focus on God. Remember, that is what true worship is all about: pouring your whole being into worshiping God.

Individual Worship

Beyond the corporate worship service, it is important to adopt an attitude of worship throughout the week. In Hebrews 13:15 we are instructed to "continually offer a sacrifice of praise to God." How can we do this? As you go through your day, sense God's presence and praise him for what you see and experience, whether it's a beautiful sunrise, the joy of a hug from a friend or a child, or the soft breeze whispering through the leaves. Listen to Christian music, and sing along. Have an attitude of expectancy, looking for God's presence and God's activity in every activity and experience of the day.

Worship also involves surrendering our lives to God's will. Romans 12:1 puts it this way: "Present your bodies as a living sacrifice, holy and acceptable to God, which is your spiritual worship." This means that worship permeates *everything* we do as Christians. In everything we do, we are to do it as if we are doing it for the Lord (Ephesians 6:7). Christ becomes the focus of our whole lives. That is the real meaning of worshiping him in "spirit and in truth."

5. Service

You, my brothers [and sisters], were called to be free. But do not use your freedom to indulge the sinful nature; rather, serve one another in love. (Galatians 5:13 NIV)

In this passage from Galatians, the instruction to serve one another in love is not a suggestion; it is a command. Jesus said that even he, the Messiah, "did not come to be served, but to serve" (Mark 10:45 NIV). In fact, Jesus said that he *expects* us to serve one another. In the thirteenth chapter of John, after he has washed the disciples' feet, Jesus says: "You call me Teacher and Lord—and you are right, for that is what I am. So if I, your Lord and the Teacher, have washed your feet, you also ought to wash one another's feet. For I have set you an example that you also should do as I have done to you" (v. 13-15). Jesus set the example we are to follow.

An attitude of humility is important here. Paul said that we are to take on the attitude of Christ, who "although he was in the form of God, did not regard equality with God as something to be exploited, but emptied himself, taking the form of a slave" (Philippians 2:5-7). Jesus himself told the disciples many times that they should have a servant's heart and attitude. When the disciples argued about which of them was the greatest, Jesus chastised them. He said, "You know that among the Gentiles those whom they recognize as their rulers lord it over them; and their great ones are tyrants over them. But it is not so among you; but whoever wishes to become great among you must be your servant; and whoever wishes to be first among you must be slave of all" (Mark 10:42-44).

Humility is difficult for us; we all struggle against pride. Yet God loves a humble heart. Proverbs 16:5 says, "Everyone who is proud in heart is an abomination to the LORD" (NASB). We want to please God, but we cannot defeat pride on our own. Only through the power of the Holy Spirit are we able to gain a servant's humble heart. The discipline of service—service for which we do not seek recognition—helps in that battle. John Ortberg writes that we should serve not as super-Christians serving those less spiritual than ourselves, but as "a society of sinners helping each other" (*The Life You've Always Wanted: Spiritual Disciplines for Ordinary People* [Grand Rapids: Zondervan, 1997] p. 109).

The discipline of service is something that should pervade our lives. It is not only action, but also attitude. It takes the form of little services for others, such as doing something without being asked, or doing something for someone without telling him or her—or anyone else—who did it, as Jesus suggested in Matthew 6:3-4. Sometimes it is simply being available and willing to listen to someone who needs to talk. Another way to serve others is to be respectful of all of God's children by refusing to listen to gossip about someone and, instead, speaking only positive words, protecting his or her reputation. There are countless opportunities for serving others each and every day.

6. Fasting

Then I turned to the Lord God, to seek an answer by prayer and supplication with fasting…. (Daniel 9:3)

Fasting is abstaining from something. Typically, this is food of some kind, but it can take the form of other things we enjoy. The purpose is not to punish ourselves by avoiding things that bring us pleasure, but to temporarily remove those things that distract us from seeking God. Fasting helps us focus on God, seeking his guidance. It is a time of intentional focus on God, waiting attentively for his direction.

Unfortunately, fasting has a somewhat negative connotation in today's society. Sometimes fasting is associated with extremism or activism. More often, however, we are simply too self-centered to fast. We are more concerned about self-fulfillment than surrender. We want what we want when we want it—instant gratification of all our desires.

Yet, fasting is a timeless discipline that does have a place in our lives today. Though fasting was an important method of seeking God in Old Testament times, in Jesus' day, and in the early church, it may be even more beneficial for us today than in times past. Think about it for a moment: We live in a fast-paced global society, with instant information and abounding distractions. Fasting helps us temporarily "unplug" from those distractions and "plug into" God.

Fasting should always be partnered with prayer. Ask God to help you center your life on him, not on food or other distractions of the world. After all, the goal of fasting is not starvation but returning your focus to God. Fasting reminds you that it is God who sustains you spiritually. What happens spiritually during a fast is much more important than what happens to your physical body.

When you need help making an important decision, want to draw closer to God, or want guidance or direction, fasting is an appropriate discipline to employ. Whatever your reason for fasting, you can choose to fast from a single meal, to fast from all food for an entire day, or to abstain from certain foods or things for an extended period of time. This latter type of fast is often practiced during Lent, when individuals choose to give up something they enjoy, whether it is TV or chocolate or something else, for the period between Ash Wednesday and Easter. If you choose to fast from all food for a period of time, it is imperative to drink water or juice in order to prevent dehydration, which can cause severe physical problems.

Remember that fasting requires some preparation. Consult your doctor to make certain that fasting will not endanger your health. In addition, do some research on the topic. There are a number of books and websites on fasting that you might find helpful. Always use good judgment when deciding what type of fast to practice, and for how long. Remember that the purpose of fasting is not self-punishment, but seeking God.

7. Confession

If we confess our sins, he who is faithful and just will forgive us our sins and cleanse us from all unrighteousness. (1 John 1:9)

As we discussed previously, we have a tendency to wear masks with God. We are even more likely to wear our masks with one another. As Christians, we feel the need to put on a façade of righteousness. We forget that a church is not a gathering of those who have reached perfection, but a gathering of sinners. Afraid that everyone else is far more spiritual or righteous than we are, we keep our mistakes and failures to ourselves, feeling alone and isolated in our sin. Dietrich Bonhoeffer, a renowned theologian who died in a Nazi concentration camp, expressed it this way in his book *Life Together:* "Many Christians are unthinkably horrified when a real sinner is discovered among the righteous. So we remain alone with our sin, living in lies and hypocrisy…. he who is alone with his sins is utterly alone" (Bonhoeffer, Dietrich. *Life Together,* Dietrich Bonhoeffer. [San Francisco: HarperSanFrancisco Publishers, 1954] p. 110).

Confessing our sins to God is our first step, and is extremely important; it brings forgiveness and restores us to a right relationship with our Creator. Once we have admitted our sins to God in a prayer of confession, however, we still typically hide them from our brothers and sisters in Christ. Yet, by hiding our struggle with sin, we are pretending to be something we are not: perfect. Most of us acknowledge that authenticity in relationships is important. Why, then, do we hide our struggles?

For one thing, we are taught from an early age not to "air our dirty laundry." Unfortunately, pretending everything is perfect in our Christian walk stifles growth. The discipline of confession helps us accept forgiveness by removing the fear that someone will discover our sin; it also provides accountability, helping us move past guilt into transformation. Once we allow the light of Christ to shine on our mistakes, they no longer have power over us.

Confession does not have to be a formal practice, made to a member of the clergy. The discipline of confession, as we are referring to it here, is as simple as having an accountability partner—someone whom you trust enough to be totally honest with, and whom you will allow to hold you accountable for making changes in your life. We are meant to live in community with our brothers and sisters in Christ. True community means being open and authentic with one another, so we can hold each other accountable for living as we believe. In James, we are instructed to be honest about our failings with one another: "Confess your sins to one another, and pray for one another, so that you may be healed (5:16). Likewise, in Galatians 6:1, Paul encourages us to hold each other accountable in love, not in condemnation: "If another Christian is overcome by some sin, you who are godly should gently and humbly help that person back onto the right path. And be careful not to fall into the same temptation yourself" (NLT).

Nor does the discipline of confession require us to report every single transgression to someone. Instead, consider those big things you struggle with on a consistent basis. Perhaps it is pride, jealously, resentment, or some other less than Christ-like character trait. We all have something we struggle with overcoming in this way. In fact, we cannot do it through our own willpower. Those things can only be overcome with prayer—both our own and the prayers of another trusted believer—asking the Holy Spirit to bring transformation from the inside out!

Selecting a long-term accountability partner is a personal process. It requires a relationship with deep trust. Also important is holding the same belief and value systems. This does not mean your accountability partner has to be someone from your church or even your denomination. However, he or she should be a Christian. We also recommend you choose an accountability partner of the same gender. This provides protection from temptation and gossip, as well as a shared perspective. Finally, make sure there is an expectation not only of authenticity and accountability, but also a covenant of confidentiality in all of your discussions.

> "The discipline of confession brings an end to pretense . . . Honesty leads to confession, and confession leads to change."
>
> – Richard Foster, *Celebration of Discipline*

Final Thoughts

Thinking about practicing the spiritual disciplines can be overwhelming. Already there are more things on our "to do" lists than we can handle! How can we possibly succeed at all of these disciplines?

The truth of the matter is that practicing spiritual disciplines is a journey, just as our faith walk is a journey. Sometimes we'll take two steps forward and then three steps back. That's okay! We should start small, adding more when we're ready. Once we're practicing the disciplines regularly, we still will have some periods of spiritual "dryness." Even the most mature Christians have them. Our relationship with God is like our relationship with other people in this way: There are natural ebbs and flows. If we continue to seek God through the disciplines, as well as through fellowship with the community of faith, eventually the flow will begin again.

As you become more accustomed to practicing the disciplines, don't let your practice lead you to become a modern day Pharisee— "holier than thou" or legalistic. Remember that the faith journey is a personal one. Encourage others along their journeys rather than judging them for not progressing as fast or as far as you. After all, God made each of us unique, and our unique personalities cause us to relate to God in different ways and at different rates. As Gary Thomas writes in his book *Sacred Pathways*, "What feeds one doesn't feed all" ([Grand Rapids: Zondervan Publishing House, 2000] p. 17). This is why some of the disciplines may attract you, while others may seem like work. This also applies to how you practice each of the disciplines. Certain types of prayer, study, or worship may appeal to you more than others. The key is to find what works for you, and then do it. Keep it real, not ritual! The attitude with which we practice the disciplines is as important as the practice itself.

Biblical Foundation

As you review each Scripture passage, underline or circle key words or phrases. Think about the implications of each passage for your life, noting your insights in the space provided. Answer the questions that follow.

Prayer

Let us therefore approach the throne of grace with boldness, so that we may receive mercy and find grace to help in time of need. (Hebrews 4:16)

"And whenever you pray, do not be like the hypocrites; for they love to stand and pray in the synagogues and at the street corners, so that they may be seen by others. Truly I tell you, they have their reward. But whenever you pray, go into your room and shut the door and pray to your Father who is in secret; and your Father who sees in secret will reward you. When you are praying, do not heap up empty phrases as the Gentiles do; for they think that they will be heard because of their many words. Do not be like them, for your Father knows what you need before you ask him." (Matthew 6:5-8)

Study

Continue in the…sacred writings that are able to instruct you for salvation through faith in Christ Jesus. All Scripture is inspired by God and useful for teaching, for reproof, and for correction, and for training in righteousness; so that everyone who belongs to God may be

proficient, equipped for every good work. (2 Timothy 3:14-17)

"For the overseer must be above reproach as God's steward…holding fast the faithful word which is in accordance with the teaching, so that he will be able both to exhort sound doctrine and to refute those who contradict." (Titus 1:7, 9 NASB)

Solitude and Simplicity

Be still, and know that I am God! (Psalm 46:10a)

"No one can serve two masters; for either he will hate the one and love the other, or he will be devoted to one and despise the other. You cannot serve God and wealth." (Matthew 6:24 NASB)

Worship

Because your steadfast love is better than life, my lips will praise you. So I will bless you as long as I live; I will lift up my hands and call on your name. (Psalm 63:3-4)

Make a joyful noise to the Lord, all the earth. Worship the Lord with gladness; come into his presence with singing…Enter his gates with thanksgiving and his courts with praise. Give thanks to him, bless his name. (Psalm 100:1-2, 4)

Service

Therefore I urge you, brethren, by the mercies of God, to present your bodies a living and holy sacrifice, acceptable to God, which is your spiritual service of worship. (Romans 12:1 NIV)

Whatever you do, do your work heartily, as for the Lord rather than for [people], knowing that from the Lord you will receive the reward of the inheritance. It is the Lord Christ whom you serve. (Colossians 3:23-24 NASB)

"Truly I say to you, to the extent that you [serve] one of these brothers [or sisters] of mine, even the least of them, you did it to me." (Matthew 25:40 NASB)

Fasting

"Then I turned to the Lord God, to seek an answer by prayer and supplication with fasting…" (Daniel 9:3)

"Whenever you fast, do not look dismal, like the hypocrites do, for they disfigure their faces so as to show others that they are fasting. Truly I tell you, they have received their reward. But when you fast, put oil on your head and wash your face so that your fasting may be seen not by others, but by your Father who is in secret; and your Father who sees in secret will reward you." (Matthew 6:16-18)

Confession

Therefore, confess your sins to one another, and pray for one another, so that you may be healed. (James 5:16a)

Reflection Questions

1. Are there any common themes in attitude or approach toward the disciplines in the preceding passages?

2. According to these passages, what is the purpose of the disciplines?

3. What required procedures or personal qualifications are needed before we can practice the disciplines?

 # HEART

Taking It to Heart

1. Assess where you are today in your relationship with Christ. Plot it on the graph below:

_____

Almost Strangers   Intimate Friendship

2. Assess where you are today in practicing spiritual disciplines. Plot the frequency with which you practice each discipline on the appropriate graph:

Prayer:

_____

Rarely   Regularly

Study:

_____

Rarely   Regularly

Solitude and Simplicity:

_____

Rarely   Regularly

Worship:

_____

Rarely   Regularly

Service:

_____

Rarely   Regularly

Fasting:

_____

Rarely   Regularly

Confession:

_____

Rarely   Regularly

3. Which disciplines "feed" you? Which ones do you find most nourishing and fulfilling? Why?

4. Which ones do not excite or fulfill you? Why?

5. What obstacles have you faced in practicing spiritual disciplines?

Heart to Heart

1. As a group, develop a two- to three-sentence summary of the video presentation.

2. Discuss the Scripture passages from this week's reading. Which one(s) spoke to you? Why?

3. Share your experiences with spiritual disciplines. Are there any you practice on a regular basis? What's your routine? Note that the routine "looks" different for each person. Why do you think this is so?

4. What's life like when you feel most connected to God? How does that impact your daily routine? What about when you feel distanced from God?

5. Discuss the obstacles you have faced in practicing spiritual disciplines. What can you do to overcome them?

HANDS

Action Plan

1. Before you begin your action plan for the coming week, get with your accountability partner(s) and spend approximately one minute each sharing your progress on last week's action plan.

2. What life changes might you need to make in order to make spiritual disciplines a regular part of your life?

3. Select one spiritual discipline to focus on over the next week. Complete the following to create an action plan for practicing this discipline each day.

Which discipline did you select?

When will you practice it? How often?

How will you do it?

Why did you choose this discipline?

Write a commitment statement, describing what you plan to do over the next week as you practice this discipline.

Share your action plan and commitment statement with your accountability partner(s). Next week you'll share your progress, including what worked and what didn't.

SESSION 3

ABIDING IN THE VINE
Growing Toward Spiritual Maturity

Materials Needed:

◆ nametags
◆ pens or pencils
◆ TV and DVD player

For opening activity:
◆ blank sheet of paper for each group

Room Set-up:

◆ Arrange pre-assigned groups around tables so that members are facing one another.
◆ Place TV and DVD player so that all can see (participants may need to turn their chairs around to view video).

Timing:

This outline is designed to cover a ninety-minute session. If you prefer to fit this into a sixty-minute format, we suggest deleting the Opening Activity and reducing the Heart to Heart Small Group Discussion to thirty minutes and the Hands Action Plan to ten minutes. If you prefer a two-hour format, include a fifteen-minute break after the Video Presentation Discussion, and add fifteen minutes to the Heart to Heart Small Group Discussion.

Opening Prayer and Welcome

(5 minutes)

Welcome participants to Leadership from the Heart, Session 3. The purpose of this session is to discover that reaching spiritual maturity is a lifelong journey that can be achieved only through an abiding (continuous), close relationship with Jesus Christ.

Opening Activity

(10 minutes)

*Do not share the purpose of this activity with participants until after the activity is completed. Doing so will undermine the process of self-discovery, which is important for adult learning.

The purpose of this activity is to help participants realize that their journey toward spiritual maturity will have ups and downs, but if they abide in Christ, they will still experience forward progress.

Ask each small group to list on a sheet of paper the major milestones of human development from birth through adulthood. Examples might include the "terrible twos," puberty, a first date, and so forth. Allow three minutes for them to complete the assignment.

Bring the full group back together and have participants call out stages they've listed. Encourage members of all small groups to participate. Allow two minutes for this.

Use the following questions to generate a short discussion (allow five minutes for this):

1. What did you notice about human development?
2. When you consider human development, how does it compare to our spiritual development?
3. How can we apply these insights to our daily lives, especially in regard to spiritual maturity?

Video Presentation

Jeff Kirby (Approx. 10 minutes)

Play the video segment for Session 3.

Full Group Video Discussion

(5 minutes)

Facilitate a full group discussion based on the video presentation using the questions that follow. Don't be nervous if no one responds immediately. If there is a pause and you do not fill in the silence, some eventually will speak up! After someone responds, ask for other comments. After one or two comments, go on to the next question, and so forth. Try to keep this initial discussion brief and to the point. Inform the participants that more in-depth discussion will follow in their small groups.

1. The speaker used an image of a faucet that continually pours water to illustrate the abiding presence of the Holy Spirit. What are your thoughts on that image?
2. Soren Kierkegaard said, "The Bible is a letter from God with our personal addresses on it." How does that make you feel?
3. As the speaker mentioned, the phrase "one another"—as in "love one another," "encourage one another," "admonish one another," and so forth—occurs more than two hundred times in the Bible. What does that say to you?

Bring the group back to this key point:

> *Reaching spiritual maturity is a process, a lifelong journey, not an event. We'll have ups and downs, but we must never give up!*

Heart to Heart Small Group Discussions

(40 minutes)

Each small group guide should start the discussion by reminding group members that the discussion questions are not designed to have "right" or "wrong" answers. They are meant to encourage group members to share their own insights and experiences, as well as what they've learned, so that members of the group can learn from one another. Everyone has something to offer! The guide should encourage each person to participate, and

should keep any one individual from dominating the discussion. Refer to the Tips for Small Group Guides in this Leader's Guide (page 8) for pointers on group facilitation.

Begin by asking the group to summarize the video presentation. Groups should try to get that message into a few short sentences.

Ask group members which passage(s) from this week's Scripture spoke to them and why.

Continue the discussion using the Heart to Heart questions on page 44.

Hands Action Plan

(15 minutes)

Small group guides should direct group members to get with their accountability partner(s) and proceed with the Hands portion of the session on page 45.
First, they each take one minute reporting their progress on last week's action plan. What did and did not happen as they had hoped?

Next, they take six to eight minutes developing their action plans for this week.

Finally, each one shares his or her action plan for the upcoming week.

Closing Circle Prayer

(5 minutes)

Small group guides should bring the accountability partners of the small groups back together for joys and concerns and a closing prayer. Ask the participants to keep their comments brief, encouraging them to share detailed prayer requests outside of class time— either in person, on the phone, or via email.

We encourage you to use a circle prayer format to close the small group time. The ability to lead a group in prayer is essential in Christian leadership, but many people are not comfortable praying aloud. Circle prayers are useful in helping people become comfortable praying in a group. Remind the participants that their words do not have to be elaborate— just from the heart!

Have members stand, if they are able, holding hands around the table. Ask each person to speak one sentence in prayer, with the small group guide opening and closing the prayer.

ABIDING IN THE VINE
Growing Toward Spiritual Maturity

"I am the true vine, and my Father is the vinegrower...Abide in me as I abide in you. Just as the branch cannot bear fruit by itself unless it abides in the vine, neither can you unless you abide in me. I am the vine, you are the branches. Those who abide in me and I in them bear much fruit, because apart from me you can do nothing."

(John 15:1, 4-5)

 HEAD

Key Insights

◆ The result of an abiding relationship with Christ through the spiritual disciplines is *transformation*.

◆ Transformation is evidenced by 1) our growth toward spiritual maturity and 2) the fruit we bear for the kingdom of God.

Understanding the Concept

In John 15, Jesus says that he is the vine and we are the branches. This metaphor implies that it is through Christ that we receive strength and nourishment. Without his sustenance, we cannot produce fruit. The term "fruit" refers to results, both *in* us—our transformation toward Christ-likeness— and *through* us—the impact we have for God's kingdom through the use of our spiritual gifts. Our focus in this chapter is the fruit of inward transformation, or spiritual maturity, which is the primary fruit of the spiritual disciplines. In the next chapter we will explore the fruit produced through the use of our spiritual gifts.

Spiritual maturity is a term that is often misunderstood. It is not being perfect. It is not being a Bible scholar or a "super-Christian" who is active in every volunteer position available. In fact, it is not even a destination we can fully reach in this life. Rather, it is a journey that lasts our whole lives as we learn to abide in Christ. (We'll explore what it

means to "abide in Christ" later.) Simply put, spiritual maturity is becoming more and more like Christ.

Spiritual Maturity Is Becoming More Like Christ

In his letters, the Apostle Paul told the early Christians that the goal of the Christian life is to be transformed. To the church at Ephesus, he wrote, "You were taught, with regard to your former way of life, to put off your old self, which is being corrupted by its deceitful desires; to be made new in the attitude of your minds; and to put on the new self, created to be like God in true righteousness and holiness" (Ephesians 4:22-24 NIV). In other words, we are to take on the character of Christ. Yet, how can this happen? After all, our natural human character is self-centered, not God-centered. Taking on the character of Christ requires change, but this is not something we can do on our own.

The good news is that *God is capable of changing us.* Think about the great leaders in the Bible. Many of them needed change. Moses was a murderer; David was an adulterer *and* a murderer. Peter denied Christ three times, yet Christ chose him to lead the early church. Paul was a persecutor of the early church, yet God transformed him into its greatest evangelist. Paul himself tells us how this transformation happens in his second letter to the Corinthians: "As the Spirit of the Lord works within us, we become more and more like [Christ] and reflect his glory even more" (3:18b NLT).

As Christians, we are to become more like Christ by taking on the character of Christ. This occurs through the process of spiritual growth; and though we cannot do it by ourselves, it does require some work on our part. In Philippians 2:12, Paul encourages his readers to "work out" their salvation, signifying that although we cannot earn our salvation, a response is required on our part. We do play an active role in moving toward spiritual growth. As Rick Warren writes in his book *The Purpose Driven Life*, "Spiritual growth is not automatic. It takes an intentional commitment. You must want to grow, decide to grow, make an effort to grow, and persist in growing" ([Grand Rapids: Zondervan, 2002], p. 179). Let's consider some important points we need to remember as we commit ourselves to working toward spiritual growth.

> "God loves you just the way you are, but he refuses to leave you that way. He wants you to be just like Jesus."
>
> —Max Lucado, *Just Like Jesus*

1. Becoming Like Christ Requires a Relationship

If we want to become like Christ, we must learn to "abide in Christ." This is a term we hear often in the church, but exactly what does it mean? Abiding in Christ is following him, spending time with him, and being transformed by him as we allow the Holy Spirit to influence our values, perspectives, character, and actions. It is learning to submit our will to his as we listen to the "still, small voice" that guides us through prayer, study, worship, and the other disciplines. Simply put, it is maintaining an ongoing relationship with Christ.

The metaphor Christ gave of the vine and the branches in John 15 beautifully illustrates "abiding" as a consistent, permanent relationship. The branches are not connected to the branch *only* at fruit-bearing season. They are connected at all times, consistently drawing sustenance to *prepare* for fruit-bearing season. In his book *Just Like Jesus: Learning to Have a Heart Like His*, Max Lucado observes, "People who live long lives together eventually begin to sound alike, talk alike, and even think alike. As

we walk with God, we take on his thoughts, his principles, his attitudes. We take on his heart" ([Dallas: Word Publising, 2003], p. 61).

As a result of this ongoing relationship with Christ, we begin to adopt a distinctly Christian worldview. Our priorities start to shift away from the temporary things of the world toward the eternal things of God's kingdom. Our relationships with other people become less about our needs and more about theirs. Our responses to events and circumstances begin to be less reactive and more responsive. Our lives begin to bear the fruit of the Spirit: love, joy, peace, patience, kindness, goodness, faithfulness, gentleness, and self-control in our actions and attitudes. In essence, we begin to take on the character of Christ.

There is a woman in our congregation who exemplifies abiding in Christ. Her name is Marty. She has led numerous Bible study classes, sometimes teaching two or three on different nights of the week. Two years ago she fought a battle with cancer. Throughout her chemotherapy treatments, she remained a tower of strength and grace, always smiling. I saw her in church one Sunday, sitting with scarf over her bald scalp, and went over to give her a hug. Her first words to me were that she had heard of a death in my family, and that she was praying for me. I, who went to encourage Marty, was instead encouraged by her. Like Marty, the sustenance we receive as branches abiding in the vine of Christ strengthens us so that we can focus on the needs of others despite our own difficult circumstances.

2. Becoming Like Christ Takes Time

Becoming like Christ does not happen overnight. It takes time to reach maturity; in fact, it is a lifelong journey. There's an old saying: "Be patient with me; God isn't finished with me yet." Growing toward spiritual maturity involves admitting that we are "under construction." We will make mistakes, mess up, and, at times, exhibit very un-Christ-like behavior.

It may be encouraging to remember that we are not the first ones to struggle with the slow process of spiritual growth. The letters to the Corinthians in the New Testament were written to believers who were struggling with inflated egos, conflicts over doctrine, jealousy, and many other bad behaviors and habits. We struggle with some of these same issues, and we will continue to do so until we reach heaven. In fact, our spiritual growth tends to follow "the two steps forward, one step backward" pattern. Still, most of us expect spiritual maturity to follow a steady upward pattern such as this:

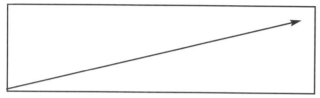

A more realistic pattern of spiritual growth looks something like this:

Actually, there are as many patterns of spiritual growth as there are people. We are all works in progress. We must recognize that each of us is on a journey toward spiritual maturity, and each of us is at a different stage in that journey.

There are seasons in our spiritual growth, too. Sometimes we will experience short but significant periods of growth; other times we will have steady periods when we are tested with opportunities to apply what we have learned; and then we will have times when we "backslide" or stumble and fall. Thankfully, our problems and failures and disappointments do not prohibit future growth but actually encourage it. In fact, sometimes we grow more through our failures than through our successes. This does not mean we excuse bad behavior; rather, we allow God to bring good from it. When others make mistakes, we forgive them and encourage them to behave differently next time. When we make mistakes, we admit our errors, ask for forgiveness, and commit to make a different decision the next time.

Actually, this is how the process of spiritual growth happens: one decision at a time. Paul explained this process when he wrote in Romans 12:2, "Do not be conformed to this world, but be transformed by the renewing of your minds, so that you many discern what is the will of God—what is good and acceptable and perfect." As we spend more time with God through Scripture study and prayer, the Holy Spirit works to enable us to recognize God's will, often through guiding our own internal conversations and thoughts. We begin to understand what he wants us to do—and not to do—and gradually our decisions come more in line with his will as revealed through the Bible. The key word here is *gradually*. It may even seem like we are not growing at all. The truth is that the more mature our faith is, the more aware we are of our own failings. Sometimes the only way to see how much we have grown is to consider where we started and how far we have come.

The good news is that regardless how slow our growth is, or how messy the path we take toward maturity, God will not give up on us. In Philippians 1:6, Paul states it this way: "I am confident of this, that the one who began a good work among you will bring it to completion by the day of Jesus Christ."

3. Becoming Like Christ Is Painful

Sometimes we fall into the trap of thinking that once we accept Christ, everything in life should go smoothly for us. We need to remember, however, that God's ultimate goal for our lives is not our comfort, but our transformation. Jesus' death on the cross was meant to achieve a far-reaching purpose: to change our hearts. The goal was not to make us happy or to provide for our physical comfort, but to enable us to say, in the words of the old hymn, "It is well with my soul" despite the troubles or trials we may face.

Jesus told his disciples they would face persecution and suffering: "They will arrest you and persecute you…you will be betrayed even by parents and brothers, by relatives and friends, and they will put some of you to death. You will be hated by all because of my name" (Luke 21:12a, 16-17). He also said that those who wish to follow him must be willing to endure hardship and self-sacrifice: "If any want to become my followers, let them deny themselves, and take up their cross daily and follow me" (Luke 9:23).

Why would God allow us to suffer and go through trials? The point is not the suffering itself, but the change it produces in us. James encourages us with these words: "My brothers and sisters, whenever you face trials of any kind, consider it nothing but joy, because you know that the testing of your faith produces endurance; and let endurance have its full effect, so that you may be mature and complete, lacking in nothing" (James 1:2-4). Whether the trials we face are as small as denying our own worldly desires or as serious as a life-threatening illness, we know that God can bring good out of it, both in us and for us.

The Apostle Paul faced many trials—he was beaten, imprisoned, shipwrecked, and finally martyred—yet he had this attitude: "I regard everything as loss because of the surpassing value of knowing Christ Jesus my Lord. For his sake I have suffered the loss of all things, and regard them as rubbish in order that I may gain Christ" (Philippians 3:8). He wrote this to the Romans: "We also rejoice in our sufferings, because we know that suffering produces perseverance; perseverance, character; and character, hope" (5:3-4 NIV). Paul knew that when we have an abiding relationship with Christ and allow the Holy Spirit to guide us, we are able to respond to problems with faith in spite of fear, with love instead of bitterness, and with gentleness instead of anger. Then, even life's difficulties can become experiences leading to spiritual growth. Perhaps Paul explained it best when he wrote to the Philippians: "I have learned to be content in whatever circumstances I am. I know how to get along with humble means, and I also know how to live in prosperity; in any and every circumstance I have learned the secret of being filled and going hungry, both of having abundance and suffering need. I can do all things through him who strengthens me (4:11b-13 NASB).

4. Becoming Like Christ Involves Others

Another way we become like Christ is through our fellowship with other Christians. God often works or speaks through others to shape our character, making us more like Christ. When we practice authenticity in our relationships with other Christians, we allow them to see our mistakes and trust them for support and encouragement as we grow toward maturity. Likewise, we learn and grow by watching their example. Remember, even Jesus sent the disciples out in pairs so they did not journey alone.

Paul often uses an analogy of the human body to illustrate this concept, calling the church the Body of Christ, and Christians, members of the body. He says that we need one another, just as the human body needs all the individual parts in order to function most effectively. In his first letter to the Corinthians, he explains why: "[So] that there may be no dissension within the body, but the members may have the same care for one another. If one member suffers, all suffer together with it; if one member is honored, all rejoice together with it. Now you are the body of Christ, and individually members of it" (1 Corinthians 12:25-27).

As members of the Body of Christ, we are called to encourage and help one another on our faith journeys. In his letter to the Colossians, Paul writes: "Let the word of Christ dwell in you richly; teach and admonish one another in all wisdom" (3:16a). Likewise, in his first letter to the Thessalonians, Paul instructs believers to "encourage one another and build up each other" (5:11a). We cannot grow to spiritual maturity in isolation. We were designed to grow in community.

5. Becoming Like Christ Equips Us to Lead

As we have mentioned, spiritual maturity takes time. It is a process, a journey. Although this journey is different for every individual, there are basically three broad stages involved. First is the Seeker stage, when we are trying to learn more about Christianity. Then comes the Explorer stage, when we commit to following Christ and to growing in our faith. Finally, there is the Guide stage, when we are becoming deeply committed Christians—not only dedicated to following Christ ourselves, but also to guiding or leading others in the faith. It is this final stage that is critical to Christian leadership. Christian leadership in the church has a two-fold purpose; it has a practical side and a spiritual side. On the practical side, Christian leadership involves providing vision and direction, empowering others to get things done, encouraging them when things seem tough, and cheering them on during success. The more important purpose, though, is the spiritual side, which involves guiding others toward spiritual maturity. As leaders in the church, pursuing spiritual maturity is crucial, because we cannot lead people to where we are not headed ourselves!

Christian leadership is leadership "in the name of Christ." In ancient times, a person's name identified something about his or her character. So, if we are to lead "in the name of Christ," we are to lead with Christ-like character. Leading with Christ-like character is possible only if we are abiding in Christ and growing toward spiritual maturity. As Christian leaders, we must be open to receiving guidance through Scripture and prayer, building authenticity in relationships, and giving all the glory for accomplishments to God. Christian leadership is not about becoming a superstar, but about being a servant.

The concept of servant-leadership, however, is contrary to much of what we are taught about leadership in the secular world. Often secular leadership revolves around an individual's dynamic personality, persuasiveness, and abilities. servant-leadership goes against our natural human tendency to seek approval, acceptance, and accolades. Servant-leaders follow the model for leadership given by Christ. We do this by abiding in Christ and allowing him to transform our leadership from seeking to gain glory and power to seeking to give glory to God and bear fruit for his kingdom.

This paraphrase of 1 Corinthians 13 superbly illustrates the importance of a vital, healthy relationship with God to our ability to lead, and serves as a fitting conclusion to our exploration of spiritual maturity:

If I cast vision with the tongues of men and angels,
but lead without the love of God at my core,
I am a ringing cell phone or worse, a clamoring vacuous corporate type.

If I have the gift of leadership and can provide direction, build teams, and set goals,
but fail to exhibit Christ-like kindness or give Christ the credit for my accomplishments,
In the eyes of God, all my achievements count for precisely nothing.

If I give my salary to the poor, my reserved parking space… to a summer intern… ,
but neglect to relate and work in a manner worthy of the one whose name I bear,
In the final analysis, it all counts for precisely nothing.

A close, humble walk with Christ never fails. It strengthens the heart,
redirects the will, restrains the ego, and purifies the motives.
It never fails.

When I was a young leader, independent and too busy to pray,
I blew stuff up and wounded every third person I led.
But now that I am mature and have left my childish ways…I do that somewhat less!

And now these three remain: the faith to follow God boldly,
the hope to press on even when my heart is breaking,
and the love to enrich the hearts of all those I lead.

But the greatest of these is love –
the love that only comes from a quiet, close, daily walk with Christ.

(From *Courageous Leadership*, Bill Hybels [Grand Rapids: Zondervan Publishing House, 2002], p. 215)

Biblical Foundation

As you review each Scripture passage, underline or circle key words or phrases. Think about the implications of each passage for your life, noting your insights in the space provided. Answer the questions that follow.

You were taught, with regard to your former way of life, to put off your old self, which is being corrupted by its deceitful desires; to be made new in the attitude of your minds; and to put on the new self, created to be like God in true righteousness and holiness." (Ephesians 4:22-24 NIV)

As the Spirit of the Lord works within us, we become more and more like [Christ] and reflect his glory even more. (2 Corinthians 3:18b NLT)

But the fruit of the Spirit is love, joy, peace, patience, kindness, goodness, faithfulness, gentleness and self-control. (Galatians 5:22 NIV)

Don't become so well-adjusted to your culture that you fit into it without even thinking. Instead, fix your attention on God. You'll be changed from the inside out... Unlike the culture around you, always dragging you down to its level of immaturity, God brings the best out of you, develops well-formed maturity in you. (Romans 12:2 Msg.)

Since an overseer is entrusted with God's work, he must be blameless—not overbearing, not quick-tempered, not given to drunkenness, not violent, not pursuing dishonest gain. Rather he must be hospitable, one who loves what is good, who is self-controlled, upright, holy and disciplined. (Titus 1:7-8 NIV)

As God's chosen people, holy and dearly loved, clothe yourselves with compassion, kindness, and humility, gentleness and patience. Bear with each other.... Forgive as the Lord forgave you. And over all these virtues put on love, with binds them all together in perfect unity. (Colossians 3:12-14 NIV)

"By this everyone will know that you are my disciples, if you have love for one another." (John 13:35)

I urge you to live a life worthy of the calling you have received. Be completely humble and gentle; be patient, bearing with one another in love. (Ephesians 4:1-2 NIV)

Finally beloved, whatever is true, whatever is honorable, whatever is just, whatever is pure, whatever is pleasing, whatever is commendable, if there is any excellence and if there is anything worthy of praise, think about these things. Keep on doing the things that you have learned and received and heard and seen in me, and the God of peace will be with you. (Philippians 4:8-9)

Not that I...have already been made perfect, but I press on...Forgetting what is behind and straining toward what is ahead, I press on toward the goal to win the prize for which God has called me heavenward in Christ Jesus. All of us who are mature should take such a view of things. And if on some point you think differently, that too God will make clear to you. Only let us live up to what we have already attained. (Philippians 3:12-16 NIV)

Reflection Questions

1. What does Christ-like character "look like"?

2. How do we achieve Christ-like character?

3. Which of the attributes of Christ-like character do you exhibit habitually? Which ones are more of a struggle for you?

HEART

Taking It to Heart

1. Assess where you are in your journey toward spiritual maturity. Plot it on the graph below.

Seeker _____ Explorer _____ Guide ___

2. On a separate piece of paper, draw a timeline of your spiritual growth. You can do this linearly, in pictures, or however you wish. Describe yourself at various maturity points along your journey.

3. Describe some experiences that have provided opportunity for spiritual growth.

4. As you look back over your life, what sort of changes can you see in your character?

Heart to Heart:

1. As a group, develop a two- to three-sentence summary of the video presentation.

2. Discuss the Scripture passages from this week's reading. Which ones spoke to you?

3. Discuss the character attributes of a mature Christian.

4. Share your spiritual growth timeline with your group.

5. Discuss the role other Christians have played in your spiritual growth.

6. Discuss experiences of being guided by the Holy Spirit. How does the Holy Spirit encourage you to align yourself with the will of God?

7. Brainstorm together how you can be more consistent and accountable in your practice of Spiritual Disciplines.

HANDS

Action Plan

1. With your accountability partner(s), briefly share what worked and didn't work last week as you tried to follow the action plan you created to practice one spiritual discipline.

2. Complete the following to develop an *overall* action plan for personal spiritual growth.

   What character trait do you need to develop and/or strengthen?

What guidance can you find in God's Word regarding this character trait?

How can you allow the Holy Spirit to guide and direct you in this effort?

Who can you ask to support and encourage you in this effort? With whom will you practice using this character trait?

What action will you take when you stumble?

3. Write a statement describing your action plan for the next week:

4. Now share the action plan for spiritual growth you have just created with your accountability partner(s). Next week you will spend a few minutes reporting on your progress.

DISCOVERING GOD'S PLAN FOR YOUR LIFE

SESSION 4

Exploring Spiritual Gifts-Based Ministry and Personal Calling

Materials Needed:

◆ nametags
◆ pens or pencils
◆ TV and DVD player

For opening activity:
   ◆ one wire clothes hanger for each group
   ◆ blank sheet of paper for each group

Room Set-up:

Arrange pre-assigned groups around tables so that members are facing one another. Place TV and DVD player so that all can see (participants may need to turn their chairs around to view video).

Timing:

This outline is designed to cover a ninety-minute session. If you prefer to fit this into a sixty-minute format, we suggest deleting the Opening Activity and reducing the Heart to Heart Small Group Discussion to thirty minutes and the Hands Action Plan to ten minutes. If you prefer a two-hour format, include a fifteen-minute break after the Video Presentation Discussion, and add fifteen minutes to the Heart to Heart Small Group Discussion.

Opening Prayer and Welcome
(5 minutes)

Welcome participants to *Leadership from the Heart*, Session 4. The purpose of this session is to understand that God has uniquely gifted us in accordance with his plan for our lives, and that, as leaders, we are called to promote a culture in our churches that values gifts-based ministry.

Opening Activity
(10 minutes)

*Do not share the purpose of this activity with participants until after the activity is completed. Doing so will undermine the process of self-discovery, which is important for adult learning.

The purpose of this activity is to help participants realize that although we may be capable of serving in a wide variety of ways (just as a hanger can be used in many ways), we will be most effective when serving in the manner God intended, according to our spiritual gift(s).

Give each group a wire hanger and a blank sheet of paper, challenging them to list all the ways a wire hanger can be used. Allow three minutes for them to complete the assignment.

Bring the full group back together and have participants call out the uses for a wire hanger that they've listed. Encourage members of all small groups to participate. Allow three minutes for this.

Use the following questions to generate a short discussion (allow four minutes for this):

1. What were your insights from this exercise?
2. How do those insights relate to our spiritual gifts? *Point out that, like the hanger, we are capable of doing many things, but we are most effective at doing what we were created to do.*
3. How can we apply these insights to our daily lives?

Video Presentation
Yvonne Gentile (Approx. 8 minutes)

Play the video segment for Session 4.

Full Group Video Discussion
(5 minutes)

Facilitate a full group discussion based on

the video presentation using the questions that follow. Don't be nervous if no one responds immediately. If there is a pause and you do not fill in the silence, someone eventually will speak up! After someone responds, ask for other comments. After one or two comments, go on to the next question, and so forth. Try to keep this initial discussion brief and to the point. Inform the participants that more in-depth discussion will follow in their small groups.

1. The speaker stated that God designed the church to function with each person using his or her gifts in service to the whole body. Why do you think God designed it that way?
2. She said that leaders need to create a culture that values gifts-based ministry and the concept of "every person is a minister." What are some specific things you could do to make that happen?
3. What other insights did you glean from this video?

Bring the group back to this key point:
  Spiritual gifts-based ministry is God's plan for how the church should function. As leaders, we are called to model gifts-based ministry, encourage others to discover and use their gifts, and affirm the gifts we see in action.

Heart to Heart Small Group Discussions

(40 minutes)

Each small group guide should start the discussion by reminding group members that the discussion questions are not designed to have "right" or "wrong" answers. They are meant to encourage group members to share their own insights and experiences, as well as what they've learned, so that members of the group can learn from one another. Everyone has something to offer! The guide should encourage each person to participate, and should keep any one individual from dominating the discussion. Refer to the Tips for Small Group Guides section in this *Leader's Guide* (page 8) for pointers on group

facilitation.

Begin by asking the group to summarize the video presentation. Groups should try to get that message into a few short sentences.

Ask group members which passage(s) from this week's Scripture spoke to them and why.

Continue the discussion using the Heart to Heart questions on page 55.

Hands Action Plan

(15 minutes)

Small group guides should direct group members to get with their accountability partner(s) and proceed with the Hands portion of the session on page 55.

First, they each take one minute reporting their progress on last week's action plan. What did and did not happen as they had hoped?

Next, they take six to eight minutes developing their action plans for this week.

Finally, each one shares his or her action plan for the upcoming week.

Closing Circle Prayer

(5 minutes)

Small group guides should bring the accountability partners of the small groups back together for joys and concerns and a closing prayer. Ask the participants to keep their comments brief, encouraging them to share detailed prayer requests outside of class time— either in person, on the phone, or via e-mail.

We encourage you to use a circle prayer format to close the small group time. The ability to lead a group prayer is essential in Christian leadership, but many people are not comfortable praying aloud. Circle prayers are useful in helping people become comfortable praying in a group. Remind the participants that their words do not have to be elaborate— just from the heart!

Have members stand, if they are able, holding hands around the table. Ask each person to speak one sentence in prayer, with the small group guide opening and closing the prayer.

CHAPTER 4

DISCOVERING GOD'S PLAN FOR YOUR LIFE
Exploring Spiritual Gifts-Based Ministry and Personal Calling

"Do not neglect the [spiritual] gift that is in you..." (1 Timothy 4:14a)

Note: This chapter is written with the assumption that you have an understanding of spiritual gifts, including an awareness of your own giftedness. If not, you will want to read a book on spiritual gifts, such as *Serving from the Heart: Finding Your Gifts and Talents for Service,* and use the questionnaire or tool provided to identify your gifts.

 HEAD

Key Insights

◆ Every leader in the church has three key responsibilities related to spiritual gifts (see "Understanding the Concept").

◆ Developing and using the spiritual gifts and special abilities God has given you is both an obligation and a privilege.

◆ God has a specific purpose and plan—or calling—for every person; discovering and fulfilling that calling is a lifelong process.

◆ Helping others to recognize, develop, and use their spiritual gifts transforms lives and multiplies the work of the kingdom.

◆ One of the most effective ways to serve in harmony with God's plan for the church is through a spiritual gifts-based ministry.

Understanding the Concept

There are many different definitions of leadership. For the purpose of this study, we are defining it simply as guiding and influencing others.

Though the number of individuals you guide and the degree of your influence may vary greatly from that of other leaders, this is actually irrelevant to the *art of leadership.* There also are many different approaches to leadership. Every individual brings his or her own personality and experiences to the role of leadership. Regardless of these differences, *everyone* God calls to a position of leadership in the church has three key responsibilities:

1) To be a good steward of your spiritual gifts and personal calling.
2) To recognize and celebrate the gifts God has given others.
3) To serve in harmony with God's plan for the church.

Let's look at each of these responsibilities separately.

1. Being a Good Steward of Your Spiritual Gifts and Personal Calling

Your Spiritual Gifts

Just as you are to be a good steward of your material resources, you also are to be a good steward of the spiritual gifts God has given you. By definition, *spiritual gifts* are "special (divine) abilities given to every Christian, by the grace of God, through the Holy Spirit, to be used to serve and strengthen one another, and to glorify God" (*Serving from the Heart: Finding Your Gifts and Talents for Service*, Carol Cartmill and Yvonne Gentile [Nashville, TN: Abingdon Press, 2002] p. 17). Examples of specific spiritual gifts are administration, encouragement, evangelism, giving, helps, leadership, mercy, teaching, and pastor-teacher (sometimes referred to as the "shepherding" gift). If you have not already completed a study of spiritual gifts, such as *Serving from the Heart*, you are encouraged to do so. In addition to helping you find your own personal calling, knowledge of spiritual gifts equips you to encourage others in their search for meaningful, purposeful service.

The spiritual gift of *leadership* is the divine ability to motivate, coordinate, and direct people doing God's work. Individuals with the gift of leadership are visionaries who inspire others to work together to make a vision become reality. They take responsibility for setting and achieving goals and are willing to step in where needed. They work to build a capable team, and then they empower that team. They are servant-leaders who live by a high moral standard and lead by their own example.

Has God spiritually gifted you to be a leader? This may be a difficult question to answer. All believers have received at least one spiritual gift, and some have received spiritual gifts through which the Holy Spirit divinely equips us specifically for leadership. If this is the case with you, you are obligated to develop and use your leadership gifting, just as you are to steward any and all of the other spiritual gifts you have received. If you are like many servant-leaders, you may have other primary gifts such as apostleship, administration, evangelism, pastor-teacher, prophecy, or teaching.

While some of us have been *gifted* by God to be leaders, others of us find ourselves in situations where we feel *compelled* to provide leadership. In his book *A Fish Out of Water*, George Barna writes that "there are two types of leaders: those who are called

and gifted by God to lead other people and cannot help but be a leader under pressure, and those who lead only because they are forced to in a given situation" ([Nashville, TN: Integrity Publishers, 2002] p. 21). Whether you are a "natural born" leader (of which there are very few), a spiritually gifted leader (a few more, but still a minority), or one who finds yourself in a God-ordained situation in which you are challenged to lead, you must trust that God will equip you to effectively meet the leadership need of your particular circumstances.

As you trust in God to equip you, your part is to discover your *leadership nature*—or the unique way God has gifted *you* to lead. You see, we all approach leadership in our own unique styles, depending upon our personalities and experiences. Just as no two people are alike, no two leaders operate in exactly the same way. There are several steps to discovering your personal leadership nature. One is to complete a personality profile, which will tell you if you are, by nature, an introvert or an extrovert and will help you explore your preferences in a work or service environment. Some of us prefer defined working environments while others are more spontaneous by nature. Leaders exhibit a variety of strengths, and so will you. Are you a visionary? Are you a team builder? Do you enjoy strategic planning? Are you gifted at handling details? Pay attention to your strengths and preferences. Look back at work and service experiences and reflect on your attitudes and behaviors.

Whatever your leadership nature may be, you can find joy and fulfillment in leading if you will begin to develop your strengths, shore up your weaknesses, and simply start leading the best you can, following the example of Christ. You do not

> **"Leadership, like other work of the people of faith, depends upon the vigorous and responsible use of the talents God has given to each of us. It depends upon the work of the Spirit weaving those talents into a rich tapestry. It is the marvelous and mysterious working of God through our lives and work that we call grace. Leadership is a gift from God, confirmed by the church, for the service of others and the upbuilding of the body of Christ."**
>
> ~Lovett Weems, Jr., *Church Leadership*

have to be an "expert" in order to enjoy leading others for God's purposes. In fact, whenever you are called and equipped by God to be a leader, you can be assured that your leadership is *beautiful*—a "work of heart" inspired by the love and grace of Christ. Although you may not always feel that your efforts are "beautiful," remember that "we have this treasure in clay jars, so that it may be made clear that this extraordinary power belongs to God and does not come from us" (2 Corinthians 4:7). In other words, we are all "cracked pots"! Yet, despite our imperfections, God is able to use us because of the "treasure" within us—the gifts we are given through the Holy Spirit. We can take comfort in the knowledge God is working through us to lead others.

Your Personal Calling

In their book *Discover Your Destiny*, Bill and Kathy Peel write, "If you have breath, you have a purpose" [Colorado Springs, CO: NavPress Publishing Group, 1996] p. 31). Scripture supports their claim. In John 15:16, Jesus teaches, "You did not choose me but I chose you. And I appointed you to go and bear fruit, fruit that will last." Likewise, Paul says in 2 Thessalonians, "With this in mind, we constantly pray for you, that our God may count you worthy of his calling, and that by his power he may fulfill every good purpose of yours and every act prompted by your faith" (1:11-12 NIV).

God's purpose and plan for your life are your "calling." Your calling may be your work or profession, or it may be an inner urging toward some vocation or ministry. Being a "good steward" of your calling involves discovering and pursuing God's plans for your life, which is a lifelong process. Those of us with imperfect vision wish we had 20/20 vision. If only we could see distances, whether near or far, without the benefit of special aids such as contact lenses, glasses, or binoculars. When it comes to the subject of knowing God's purpose and plan

for our lives, it would be awesome if we were given "20/20 vision." Thankfully, just as there are special tools that help us see with our eyes, there also are tools that help us discover God's plans for us. We learned about some of these tools, the spiritual disciplines, in Chapter 3. Practicing the disciplines leads us to grow in our faith; and as our faith deepens, we come to recognize God's plans for our lives and the unique "calling" God has given each of us.

As you begin to identify God's plans for your life, you may wonder how and why God would choose *you* to be a leader in the church. Take comfort and courage in the fact that God often chooses the least-likely candidates to lead his people. Just think about some of the familiar characters from the Old and New Testaments. Moses was a reluctant leader at best, called upon by God after fleeing Egypt and taking a forty-year sabbatical in the desert. David was the youngest and smallest of Jesse's sons, yet God directed Samuel to anoint David as Israel's next king. Esther was only *one* of King Xerxes' many wives—and a Jew, at that—but she was God's instrument to save his chosen people from the king's death edict. Peter was arguably Jesus' most impulsive disciple, and he failed Jesus miserably by denying he even knew him; yet Peter was the "rock" upon which Jesus eventually built God's church. So, you are in good company!

God has an assignment just for you, and he is waiting for you to answer the call. Before you begin listing the reasons preventing you from answering, remember that God will equip you to effectively accomplish any assignment he may give you. God does not expect you to carry out the assignment he has given you under your own power. Rather, it is your spiritual gifting through which God's power works in your life. God only asks that you make yourself available and step out in faithful obedience. Is it risky? You bet! But you will never experience

> **"If it seems that [God] has ordained you to serve people through leadership, accept the challenge and invest yourself in being the best leader you can be."**
>
> —George Barna, *A Fish Out of Water*

greater joy than when you discover your unique gifts and purpose, live into your calling, and experience the power and presence of God working through you to accomplish something significant for the kingdom. Then you will truly understand what it means to live life to the fullest!

Remember, however, that discovering God's purpose is a journey, and you will not always have 20/20 vision. In fact, there will be times when you will only be able to take one step at a time. Still, you always can rely on God's promises and trust him to show you the way. Take to heart this reassurance of Jesus: "Peace I leave with you; my peace I give to you. I do not give to you as the world gives. Do not let your hearts be troubled and do not let them be afraid" (John 14:27).

2. Recognizing and Celebrating the Gifts God Has Given Others

Your second responsibility as a leader in the church is to affirm the gifts you see in others. This is not only a duty of servant-leadership; it also is a privilege. Think for a moment about a time when someone recognized in you a God-given gift or ability. How did you feel? As a leader, you will be given numerous opportunities to impact others in the same way.

As you serve with others, ask God in prayer to reveal to you their unique gifts and abilities. Observe what is happening while they are serving. Look for specific details; then use those details in recognizing their service. For example, you may have the opportunity to watch someone lead a children's Sunday school class. Later you might describe for the individual the reactions of the children and the results of the teaching. Depending on the situation, you might say something such as, "I was watching the children while you were reading the Bible story, and they looked so interested and happy. I know your teaching reminded them of Jesus' love."

The deeper your knowledge about spiritual gifts, the better equipped you will be to name the spiritual gifts you observe in action. By sharing this information, you are opening the door to learning for others, perhaps encouraging them to learn about spiritual gifts for themselves. As this happens, your entire church will benefit as more and more members discover and begin to use their God-given gifts.

3. Serving in Harmony with God's Plan for the Church

A third responsibility you have as a leader in the church is to honor and actively participate in God's plan for the church. In the book of Romans, Paul describes this plan with the analogy of the human body. He writes, "Just as each of us has one body with many members, and these members do not all have the same function, so in Christ we who are many form one body, and each member belongs to all the others" (Romans 12:4-5 NIV).

The human body is healthiest when all its members are actively engaged, functioning in the roles for which they were designed. So, too, the church is healthiest and primed for growth when its members have found their special places of service according to the unique ways in which God has created them. Our mouth would not be able to fulfill the needs that are met by our eyes. Our eyes fill a very specific need for our body: the need to see where we are going. We can keep moving without their help, but not as safely or efficiently. So, too, our churches are most effective as each member operates in his or her area of specific gifting. It should be the desire of every Christian for his or her church to be as effective as possible.

You see, the church is God's chosen vehicle to be his light and love in a broken world. It is special, set apart. In fact, Scripture refers to the church as the bride of Christ, and God *loves* his bride (see Ephesians 5:32 and Revelation 19:7). It stands to reason, then, that God would provide for his church and the individuals who make up the church. One way God provides is by bestowing spiritual gifts on people of faith. In his book *The Holy Spirit*, Billy Graham writes, "God did not ordain that the Church should drift aimlessly in the seas of uncertainty without compass, captain, or crew. By his Spirit he has provided for the operation of the Church in history through the gifts of his Spirit" ([Nashville: Word Publishing, 1978, 1988] p. 202).

As a servant-leader in the church, you can honor and participate in God's plan for the church by encouraging others to discover, develop, and use their spiritual gifts. By recognizing the need to invest in others so that they, too, can be released to be God's agents of healing in a broken world, you will increase the church's ability to provide meaningful ministry. In fact, your role as a leader uniquely positions you to help ensure that the church is living up to its potential. As you grasp the mission and vision of the church, you can mobilize people in a direction to fulfill both.

Spiritual gifts must become a value of the church. As more and more servant-leaders challenge and encourage people to discover and deploy their own spiritual gifts and create opportunities for people to serve, the church is better positioned to flourish. Not only are the needs of the body, the church, and its members met; the church's impact on the greater community and, ultimately, the kingdom of God, increases as well. A gifts-based ministry program is one of the most effective ways to accomplish this goal. In such a program, opportunities for studying spiritual gifts through classes, workshops, and small group studies are offered regularly. Then, after individuals discover their gifts, they are guided through a process that helps them match their gifts with places of service, with effective follow-up taking place thereafter.

As we conclude our discussion, let's briefly review some of the benefits of a spiritual gifts-based ministry:

Kingdom Benefits

Above all, God is glorified.

God's people are built up, or encouraged, in the church as gifts-based ministries are taught and developed.

People involved in meaningful service to others have a positive impact on the community.

Church Benefits

Churches with gifts-based ministries are more effective in the ministries they provide. They have people with the gift of Leadership leading, people with the gift of Helps helping, people with the gift of Mercy reaching out to people who are suffering, and so on.

Churches that teach and develop gifts-based ministries grow spiritually. When you use your gifts in service to others, you see God at work through yourself, changing lives and changing the world—one person at a time.

Personal Benefits

You will have a better understanding of God's purpose for your life. God gives each person unique gifts to fulfill God's specific plan.

Your relationship with God will grow and mature. As you minister to others and see the difference God makes in their lives through you, your relationship with God will deepen.

Your ministry will be more effective and fulfilling. For example, if you have a passion for children and the gift of Teaching, you will probably be a very effective children's Sunday school teacher. Using your gift will energize you!

Biblical Foundation

As you review each Scripture passage, underline or circle key words or phrases. Think about the implications of each passage for your life, noting your insights in the space provided. Answer the questions that follow.

> **"One definition of leadership is the ability to recognize the special abilities and limitations of others, combined with the capacity to fit each one into the job where he will do his best. He who is successful in getting things done through others is exercising the highest type of leadership."**
>
> —J. Oswald Sander, *Spiritual Leadership*

Stewardship of Your Spiritual Gifts

Do not neglect the gift that is in you, which was given to you through prophecy with the laying on of hands by the council of elders. (1 Timothy 4:14)

I remind you to rekindle the gift of God that is within you through the laying on of my hands. For God did not give us a spirit of cowardice, but rather a spirit of power and of love and of self-discipline. (2 Timothy 1:6-7)

To each is given the manifestation of the Spirit for the common good. (1 Corinthians 12:7)

Like good stewards of the manifold grace of God, serve one another with whatever gift each of you has received. Whoever speaks must do so as one speaking the very words of God; whoever serves must do so with the strength that God supplies, so that God may be glorified in all things through Jesus Christ. To him belong the glory and the power forever and ever. Amen. (1 Peter 4:10-11)

Therefore, I urge you, brothers [and sisters], in view of God's mercy, to offer your bodies as living sacrifices, holy and pleasing to God—this is your spiritual act of worship. Do not conform any longer to the pattern of this world, but be transformed by the renewing of your mind. Then you will be able to test and approve what God's will is—his good, pleasing and perfect will. For the grace given me I say to every one of you: Do not think of yourself more highly than you ought, but rather think of yourself with sober judgment, in accordance with the measure of faith God has given you. Just as each of us has one body with many members, and these members do not all have the same function, so in Christ, we who are many form one body, and each member belongs to all the others. We have different gifts, according to the grace given us. If a man's gift is prophesying, let him use it in proportion to his faith. If it is serving, let him serve; if it is teaching, let him teach; if it is encouraging, let him encourage; if it is contributing to the needs of others, let him give generously; if it is leadership, let him govern diligently; if it is showing mercy, let him do it cheerfully. (Romans 12:1-8 NIV)

Stewardship of Your Personal Calling (God's Plan and Purpose for Your Life)

As a prisoner for the Lord, then, I urge you to live a life worthy of the calling you have received. Be completely humble and gentle; be patient, bearing with one another in love. Make every effort to keep the unity of the Spirit through the bond of peace. There is one body and one Spirit—just as you were called to one hope when you were called—one Lord, one faith, one baptism, one God and Father of all, who is over all and through all and in all. (Ephesians 4:1-6 NIV)

The word of the LORD came to me, saying,
   "Before I formed you in the womb, I knew you,
      and before you were born, I consecrated you;
      I appointed you a prophet to the nations."
   (Jeremiah 1:4-5)

"For surely I know the plans I have for you," says the LORD, "plans for your welfare and not for harm, to give you a future with hope. Then when you call upon me and come and pray to me, I will hear you. When you search for, you will find me; if you seek me with all your heart." (Jeremiah 29:11-13)

As the deer longs for flowing streams, so my soul longs for you, O God. (Psalm 42:1)

For the eyes of the LORD range throughout the earth to strengthen those whose hearts are fully committed to him. (2 Chronicles 16:9a NIV)

God's Plan for the Church—the Body of Christ

You are a chosen race, a royal priesthood, a holy nation, God's own people, in order that you may proclaim the mighty acts of him who called you out of darkness into his marvelous light. (1 Peter 2:9)

The gifts he gave were that some would be apostles, some prophets, some evangelists, some pastors and teachers, to equip the saints for the work of ministry, for building up the body of Christ, until all of us come to the unity of the faith and the knowledge of the Son of God, to maturity, to the measure of the full stature of Christ. We must no longer be children, tossed to and fro and blown about by every wind of doctrine, by people's trickery, by their craftiness in deceitful scheming. But speaking the truth in love, we must grow up in every way into him who is the head, into Christ, from whom the whole body, joined and knit together by every ligament with which it is equipped, as each part is working properly, promotes the body's growth in building itself up in love. (Ephesians 4:11-16)

Reflection Questions

1. After studying these passages, what would you say is God's desire regarding the spiritual gifts given to us? List as many possible answers to this question as you are able.

2. For what purpose are spiritual gifts given?

3. What might you do to "fan into flame" the gift(s) given you?

4. What does it mean to "live a life worthy of the calling you have received"?

5. List what you learned about God's plan and purpose for your life from studying these Bible passages.

6. How do you think "seeking God with all of your heart" and "knowing the plans God has for you" relate to each other?

7. Peter describes believers as "a royal priesthood." Paul refers to believers as "the body of Christ" and teaches the importance of all the members of the body working together. Describe a church where all members contribute to its health. What does it take to make it happen, and what are the benefits?

 # HEART

Taking It to Heart

1. What are your spiritual gifts?

2. What is your leadership nature, and how might your leadership nature manifest itself? (In other words, describe the way in which you lead—I am sensitive, I encourage, I'm an organizer, etc.)

3. Describe your current service role(s). Are you using your spiritual gifts in this role? Are you using your leadership nature? If not, how can you begin to put them into action?

4. How has God worked in your life to prepare you for leadership?

5. What does the church have a "right" to expect of you? That is, if you do not do this, the chances are that no one else will because they have not been called and prepared by God to do it, or they are not currently in a position to do it.

Heart to Heart

1. As a group, develop a two- to three-sentence summary of the video presentation.

2. Share what you learned from the Scripture passages for this week about spiritual gifts and God's plan and purpose for your life.

3. Discuss God's plan for the church and our specific roles in helping his plan to be realized.

4. Tell about your spiritual gifts. If you have not completed a spiritual gifts survey and/or are unsure of your gifts, ask others to name gifts they see in you.

5. How does one acknowledge his or her spiritual gifts and remain humble? (This is not false humility.)

HANDS

Action Plan

1. With your accountability partner(s), briefly share your progress to date in carrying out the overall action plan for spiritual growth you created last week.

2. Create an action plan for further developing your *spiritual gifts* and putting them to use; then briefly share your action plan with your accountability partner(s).

3. Select two or three people you interact with on a regular basis in the church, in this group, or another Christian setting. Over the next week, through observation and listening, try to identify what their spiritual gifts are. Write a note of affirmation to each person regarding the gifts you have seen him or her using. You'll have an opportunity to discuss the experience with your accountability partner(s) next week.

LIVING THE GREAT COMMISSION

SESSION 5 Transforming Lives

Materials Needed:

◆ nametags
◆ pens or pencils
◆ TV and DVD player

For Opening Activity:
◆ one blank sheet of paper for each participant
◆ markers or crayons (optional—if you want to allow extra creativity)

Room Set-up:

◆ Arrange pre-assigned groups around tables so that members are facing one another.
◆ Place TV and DVD player so that all can see (participants may need to turn their chairs around to view video).

Timing:

This outline is designed to cover a ninety-minute session. If you prefer to fit this into a sixty-minute format, we suggest deleting the Opening Activity and reducing the Heart to Heart Small Group Discussion to thirty minutes and the Hands Action Plan to ten minutes. If you prefer a two-hour format, include a fifteen-minute break after the Video Presentation Discussion, and add fifteen minutes to the Heart to Heart Small Group Discussion.

Opening Prayer and Welcome

(5 minutes)

Welcome participants to *Leadership from the Heart*, Session 5. The purpose of this session is to understand that we are Christ's ambassadors in the world, and we have a responsibility for sharing our faith with others. As the Scripture passage in their reading says, "How will they know, if no one tells them?"

Opening Activity

(10 minutes)

Do not share the purpose of this activity with participants until after the activity is completed. Doing so will undermine the process of self-discovery, which is important for adult learning.

The purpose of this activity is to increase participants' awareness of all the people they come into contact with in the normal course of daily life. Participants will create a picture that reflects the various communities in which they participate—such as home, neighborhood/community, school, work, teams, church, and so forth.

Give each participant a blank sheet of paper. Place markers or crayons in the center of each group's table. Ask them to create a simple picture that reflects the communities of people with whom they have regular contact. They might draw themselves and immediate family members in the center and work out from there, labeling each group they draw. Allow three minutes for them to complete their pictures.

Once the pictures are done, have them indicate in some way which of the communities they drew include non-believers. In pairs, perhaps with their accountability partner, have them share thoughts and ideas of ways they might share their faith in just one of the communities. Allow three minutes for the pairs to talk, stopping halfway through to switch roles.

Bring the full group back together.

Use the following questions to generate a short discussion (allow four minutes for this):

1. Were you surprised by the number of communities reflected in your pictures?

2. What implications might this have in terms of our potential impact for the kingdom?
3. How might we begin, or continue, to be used by God to influence the people in our communities for Christ?

Video Presentation

Susan Campbell (Approx. 8 minutes)
Play the video segment for Session 5.

Full Group Video Discussion

(5 minutes)
Facilitate a full group discussion based on the video presentation using the questions that follow. Don't be nervous if no one responds immediately. If there is a pause and you do not fill in the silence, someone eventually will speak up! After someone responds, ask for other comments. After one or two comments, go on to the next question, and so forth. Try to keep this initial discussion brief and to the point. Inform the participants that more in-depth discussion will follow in their small groups.

1. What comes to mind when you think about evangelism? Why are so many of us intimidated by the thought of sharing our faith?
2. The speaker opened with a story that illustrates the powerful impact we can have in the lives of others with whom we come into contact. When you consider the people you might impact, or may already have impacted, how does that make you feel? What are your thoughts or insights about this?
3. What other insights did you glean from this video?

Bring the group back to this key point:
All Christians have a responsibility to be witnesses for Christ through our words and actions. Christ is counting on us!

Heart to Heart Small Group Discussions

(40 minutes)
Each small group guide should start the discussion by reminding group members that the discussion questions are not designed to have "right" or "wrong" answers. They are meant to encourage group members to share their own insights and experiences, as well as what they've learned, so that members of the group can learn from one another. Everyone has something to offer! The guide should encourage each person to participate, and should keep any one individual from dominating the discussion. Refer to the Tips for Small Group Guides section in this *Leader's Guide* (page 8) for pointers on group facilitation.

Begin by asking the group to summarize the video presentation. Groups should try to get that message into a few short sentences.

Ask group members which passage(s) from this week's Scripture spoke to them and why.

Continue the discussion using the Heart to Heart questions on page 68.

Hands Action Plan

(15 minutes)
Small group guides should direct group members to get with their accountability partner(s) and proceed with the Hands portion of the session on page 68.

First, they each take one minute reporting their progress on last week's action plan. What did and did not happen as they had hoped?

Next, they take six to eight minutes developing their action plans for this week.

Finally, each one shares his or her action plan for the upcoming week.

Closing Circle Prayer

(5 minutes)
Small group guides should bring the accountability partners of the small groups back together for joys and concerns and a

closing prayer. Ask the participants to keep their comments brief, encouraging them to share detailed prayer requests outside of class time— either in person, on the phone, or via e-mail.

We encourage you to use a circle prayer format to close the small group time. The ability to lead a group in prayer is essential in Christian leadership, but many people are not comfortable praying aloud. Circle prayers are useful in helping people become comfortable praying in a group. Remind the participants that their words do not have to be elaborate— just from the heart!

Have members stand, if they are able, holding hands around the table. Ask each person to speak one sentence in prayer, with the small group guide opening and closing the prayer.

LIVING THE GREAT COMMISSION
CHAPTER 5 · Transforming Lives

"Go therefore and make disciples of all nations, baptizing them in the name of the Father and of the Son and of the Holy Spirit, and teaching them to obey everything that I have commanded you. And remember, I am with you always, to the end of the age."

(Matthew 28:19-20)

 ## HEAD

Key Insights

◆ The Great Commission (Matthew 28:19-20) is a command, not a suggestion.

◆ We each have a responsibility for sharing the gospel with others.

◆ When we witness, we can rely on the power of the Holy Spirit, assured that Jesus has promised to be with us always.

◆ The only "requirement" for evangelism is our willingness.

Understanding the Concept

Why Should We Share Our Faith?

When Jesus ascended into heaven, his last words to the disciples were a command to go out and share the gospel with all nations (Matthew 28:19). The disciples were a ragtag group of uneducated, un-traveled, unpolished fellows—an unlikely group to be commissioned as ambassadors to the world. Yet they were successful beyond their wildest dreams—not because of their own abilities, but because they were willing and they relied on the power of the Holy Spirit to do the rest.

Today, Jesus is counting on *us* to be his ambassadors, especially to those people we come into contact with on a regular basis. There is an old saying, "You may be the only Bible a non-Christian ever reads." Yet, sharing our faith goes beyond living a model Christian lifestyle. It entails being willing and able to tell someone who Jesus is, why he lived, died, and rose again, and what he has done in our lives. We often call this witnessing or evangelism.

Some people shudder at the sound of the word "evangelism." For them, it carries the negative connotation of stereotypical televangelists, who often are thought of as being less than sincere—although that generalization certainly is not always true. What *is* an evangelist? The word evangelist comes to us from the Greek word *Ĕuaggĕlistēs* (yoo-ang-ghel-is-tace´), which means a preacher of the gospel. The origin of the word gospel is closely related, coming from the Greek word *Ĕuaggĕliŏn* (yoo-ang-ghel´-ee-on), which means a good message. In Acts 1:8; Jesus tells the disciples they are to be his witnesses to "the ends of the earth." The word witness comes from the Greek word *Martus (mar´-toos)*, which means a witness or a record.

So, when we say that, as Christians, we are called to evangelize or share our faith, we mean that we are expected to be witnesses about the good message of Jesus Christ. Some people think that this is a job for ordained clergy, not ordinary people. Yet, were the disciplines ordained clergy? No! They were ordinary Jews—simple men whose lives had been touched by Jesus, just as ours have been.

The disciples must have been terrified at the mere thought of being witnesses. In those days, being a follower of Jesus could lead to death. In fact, after being given this command to "go...and make disciples," they did not rush right out and start sharing the gospel. Instead, they hid because they were afraid for their lives. They forgot that Jesus had promised to be with them through the Holy Spirit and give them the courage and power to be witnesses.

The fulfillment of this promise came to pass on the day of Pentecost, fifty days after Christ's crucifixion. The disciples were gathered together when, suddenly, "from heaven there came a sound like the rush of a violent wind, and it filled the entire house where they were sitting. Divided tongues, as of fire, appeared among them, and a tongue rested on each of them. And they were all filled with the Holy Spirit" (Acts 2:2-4a). Immediately, the disciples went out into the city, telling about Jesus. In one day, three thousand people came to believe in Jesus Christ, and the church was born. After that, the disciples faced ridicule, imprisonment, and persecution, but they never refused to share their faith with the people they met. They did this not because they were gifted orators or were unafraid. This group of ordinary men was confident in sharing their faith because they trusted in the power of the Holy Spirit.

We also receive the power of the Holy Spirit when we accept Christ, and he strengthens and empowers us to share the good message of Jesus Christ. All we have to be is willing.

Why Are We Reluctant?

C.S. Lewis was once asked his opinion on Christianity's "unique contribution among world religions." his response: "Oh, that's easy. It's grace" (*What's So Amazing About Grace?* Philip Yancey [Grand Rapids: Zondervan Publishing, 1997] p. 45). Grace can be defined as getting what we need, not what we deserve. In other words, grace is God's free gift of mercy and forgiveness (what we need), not justice or punishment (what we deserve).

Some of us think we must *do* something to receive grace—that we must "be good" to get into heaven—but in our hearts, we know that we can never be "good enough," so we must trust in God and rely on his grace. The apostle Paul says it this way in Romans 3:23-24: "All have sinned and fall short of the glory of God; they are now justified by his grace as a gift, through the redemption that is in Christ Jesus."

Unfortunately, we Christians sometimes begin to think that we matter more to God than those who don't go to church, or that we are somehow "better" than they are—after all, we're doing all the "right" things: going to church, praying, reading our Bibles, and so forth. In a sense, we turn into modern day "Pharisees," thinking that, because we are believers, we are in some way more important to God than those who do not believe. This is dangerous thinking because it seeps slowly and insidiously into our hearts. The result is that we do not see the need to share our faith since we think they wouldn't understand or appreciate God's gift of grace anyway. This isn't a new way of thinking; the most "religious" people of Christ's time, the original Pharisees, thought this way, too.

We sometimes forget that Jesus spent most of his time with people outside the church: tax collectors, the poor, smelly fishermen, prostitutes, and so forth. Jesus intentionally sought out and spent time with those people for one reason: God loved them, and so they were important to him, too. In Luke 15, Jesus told three parables in response to the disdain the Pharisees were feeling because he was "hanging out" with undesirables—the Parables of the Lost Sheep, the lost coin, and the prodigal son. The whole point of these stories is that lost people matter to God, and they should matter to us, too.

If we understand that lost people matter to God and that God expects us to be witnesses to them, and if we earnestly desire to do his will, then we should be motivated to be witnesses to others. Yet, according to William Fay, author of *Share Jesus Without Fear*, less than 5-10 percent of Christians have shared their faith in the past twelve months. This number is staggering—and frightening! He suggests that if we do not witness to non-believers, and encourage everyone else in our churches to do so, too, we risk becoming "keepers of a Christian aquarium instead of fishers of men" ([Nashville: Broadman & Holman Publishers, 1999] p. 7).

Ask others why they have not shared their faith (or consider this question yourself), and you are likely to hear one of the following common reasons.

We're Afraid of Failure

We often forget that God calls us simply to share our faith, not to convert someone. We are not responsible for the person's response—only for sharing what we know and have experienced. The results are up to God. Even if a person does not accept Christ when we share our faith, we must remember that conversion is a process, and we may be moving that person one step closer to a commitment to Jesus. After all, studies have shown that the average person must hear the gospel message seven to eight times before accepting Christ.

We're Afraid of Ridicule

We all long to be accepted, and we know that sharing our faith will open us up to ridicule. Keep in mind that when people ridicule us, it is usually a defensive move. They do not want to face the conviction they are feeling about their own lives. If we share our faith with gentleness and respect, we are doing nothing of which to be ashamed. In fact, we may not even face ridicule at all. Most people, whether they agree or not, respect someone who stands up for their beliefs.

We Feel Unqualified

Often we feel inadequate. Perhaps we are afraid we won't know what to say, or we don't have enough Bible knowledge. God does not expect us all to be theologians. He just expects us to be willing. The hardest part of sharing our faith is to simply get out of the way—to leave behind our prejudices and personal agendas and let the Holy Spirit take over.

As for knowing *how to explain* the gospel message, we will share some tips later in this chapter. You might want to make notes about these tips on the inside cover of your Bible, and refer to them as needed. That is not cause for embarrassment.

We're Aware of Our Own Imperfection

Sometimes we get caught up in thinking we are not "good enough" to be witnesses for Christ. After all, we all fail to follow his teachings on occasion, and we make mistakes in our attitudes and actions. The truth is, if we have a humble attitude and make ourselves vulnerable, those mistakes might actually be the thing that causes someone to listen to our message. You don't have to be a "perfect" Christian for God to use you. That term is an oxymoron anyway, because there are no "perfect Christians." All you have to be is willing and present.

> ## "The only failure in sharing your faith is not sharing your faith at all."
> —Jim and Karen Covell, Victorya Michaels Rogers, *How To Talk About Jesus Without Freaking Out*

We Think It's Unnecessary

Many of us believe that if we just live out our faith as good examples, people will see it and be convinced they want that kind of life, too. Unfortunately, that rarely happens. What is more likely is that our example will make others more willing to *talk* to us about matters of faith—and we must be ready to do so. According to a survey from the Institute of American Church Growth, most believers become Christians (75 to 90 percent) because a friend or acquaintance talked to them about their faith (*Share Jesus Without Fear*, William Fay [Nashville: Broadman & Holman Publishers, 1999] p. 12).

We Don't Know Who to Share With

After we have been involved in church for a while, it seems everyone we know is already a believer. Actually, we should share our faith with *everyone*, even the people we meet in church! Just because someone comes to church every Sunday does not mean that he or she has made a personal decision to follow Christ. This realization is especially important to those of us who are leaders in the church. Whether we lead ministry teams, teach Bible studies, or serve in some other way, we must make sure that our ministry is sensitive to unbelievers and that we are encouraging volunteers, students, and whomever we serve—or serve with—to develop a personal relationship with Jesus.

How Can We Share Our Faith?

Recognize the Barriers

Before we begin sharing our faith with others, we need to recognize certain barriers that can prevent others from being open and willing to hear the gospel:

Pretending to Be Something We're Not

Pretending that we have it all together, or that we know it all, sets us up for failure. Let's face it: We all make mistakes. We cannot possibly live up to a perfect ideal. We will stumble on occasion. Being "real"—admitting our mistakes, asking forgiveness, and making it right—will go farther in reaching lost people than pretending we are perfect Christians.

Failing to Acknowledge Our Trials and Tribulations

We have a living relationship with God, and we have relationships with other humans. As a result, at times we feel anger, fear, disappointment, uncertainty, jealousy, worry, and sadness. Unbelievers need to see us struggle with honest emotions. They need to see us work out our faith in the midst of our problems, not pretend that faith makes problems go away.

Having faith does not mean we never worry when our circumstances are difficult or uncertain. Rather, it means we have a God who listens to our cries of distress and uncertainty. When a loved one dies, we still grieve, even if the loved one has the promise of eternal life. Yet, as Christians, we can count on God to help us weather the storm of sadness. When we struggle with anger and approach the person(s) we've hurt to apologize, asking forgiveness, we are a powerful witness to the impact faith has on a Christian's behavior. When we admit to having questions regarding our faith, a non-believer may be more likely to listen than if we pretended to have all the answers.

Pushing Too Hard, Too Soon

People are more willing to listen to, and be influenced by, people they know and trust. This means that the most effective means of evangelism is developing relationships with others and earning their trust and respect so they will be more open to listening to what we have to say.

Developing a relationship can be a slow or a quick process depending on the circumstances, but it always involves being vulnerable and willing to share openly about your own experiences. Look for opportunities to serve others, and be willing to let them serve you, too. This reciprocity will work to build a mutual relationship. Ask questions, and then really listen to the answers. There's an old saying: "No one cares what you know until they know you care." That is especially true when you are trying to witness to someone effectively.

Identify the Witnessing Style That's Right for You

It is also very important to find an approach to witnessing that fits your unique individual style. Just as each of us has a unique story, we also have a unique personality. If you are witnessing in a style that is uncomfortable for you, you may not be as effective and may not want to witness as often. On the other hand, if you witness in a manner that matches up with your individuality, you will seem more natural and feel more confident.

Here are a few witnessing styles to consider.

- *Logical.* This method uses a rational, well-organized line of reasoning to explain the gospel story, using facts and evidence to convict others of its truth. People who use this method have typically done a lot of study and are prepared to debate their points.
- *Testimonial.* This method speaks from personal experience. It is difficult for anyone to argue

with or refute someone else's personal experience. Your personal testimony is the most non-threatening method of sharing your faith. It does not have to be dramatic. What people really want to know is that God really cares and is active in your life. Even if you grew up in a Christian home and do not have a dramatic conversion story, you have gone through times of doubt or difficulty that God has carried you through.

◆ *Relational*. People who are drawn to use this method tend to be warm, people-centered individuals. They love developing relationships with unbelievers, making them part of their lives and inviting them to church and other faith-based activities.

◆ *Service*. People who naturally lean toward this approach to evangelism notice needs other people do not see and find joy in meeting them, even if they do not get any credit for it. They follow the wisdom of St. Francis of Assisi who said, "Proclaim the gospel at all times; when necessary, use words."

Be Prepared to Answer Three Questions

Whichever style of witnessing you use, there are three questions you need to be able to answer for the person with whom you are sharing your faith. This does not mean that you will need to go through all of these questions at once with that person; rather, in the process of witnessing to this person over time, these questions probably will come up in some form or fashion.

1. What has Jesus done in my own life?

This is your personal testimony—one subject on which you are the sole expert! There should be three parts to this: 1) what your life was like before you became a Christian, 2) what brought you to a decision to follow Jesus, and 3) how your life has changed since then. Ideally, you will want to be able to give your testimony in five minutes or less. The best way to prepare for this is to develop an outline, covering each of the three parts, and then practice telling it to other people. If you develop an outline instead of writing the whole story out, you will not be tempted to recite it word for word and thus seem

like you are giving a "canned" presentation; instead, the outline will serve as a guide so that you cover all the important pieces. Each time you tell it, the story will be slightly different. (You will have space to develop your outline at the end of this chapter.) Listen for clues that someone wants to hear your story. He or she may ask outright, or comment on the changes in your life or the difference in your attitude.

2. Why do we need Jesus?

There are a variety of "illustrations" or examples that will help you answer this question for people. They all point to this truth: Jesus is the only one who can solve all our problems. He justifies the sinner, loves the unloved, fills the spiritually empty, and gives meaning and purpose to those gone adrift in the sea of life. Listen for questions about how to "get" what you've found, or comments that suggest being a "good person" is enough or that "spirituality" in any form is all a person needs, which suggest that it's time to share the gospel message. The key is to keep it simple and clear. Here are few examples of illustrations you can use, though there are many more.

Roman Road: This illustration takes people through three passages in the book of Romans to show the way to salvation.

◆ All have sinned and fall short of the glory of God (Romans 3:23).
◆ For the wages of sin is death, but the free gift of God is eternal life in Christ Jesus our Lord (Romans 6:23).
◆ "Everyone who calls on the name of the Lord shall be saved" (Romans 10:13).

Do vs. Done: This illustration, from *Becoming a Contagious Christian* by Bill Hybels and Mark Mittleberg (Grand Rapids: Zondervan, 1994), is simple and easy to remember. The authors say that "religion is spelled D-O because it consists of the things people *do* to try to gain God's favor or forgiveness" (p. 155). Christianity, on the other hand, is spelled D-O-N-E because Christians believe Christ has *done* all that needs to be done for us to receive forgiveness. He died to pay the price for our sins. All we have to do is accept and follow him.

The Bridge: Developed by the Navigators, this is a frequently used illustration that is especially good to use with people who like visuals.

Start with a diagram showing God and us on opposite sides.

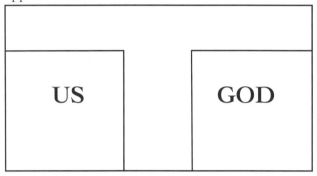

Next, add a chasm, showing how our sins have separated us from God.

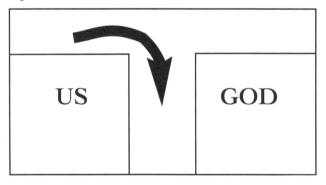

Next, add the wages of sin, DEATH, (Romans 6:23) at the bottom of the chasm, with an arrow going over our side of the chasm.

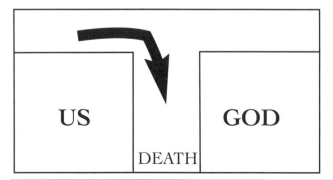

Next, cross through death, and add a cross-shaped bridge. Explain that God loves us and provided a bridge by which we can be restored to a right relationship with him. That bridge is Jesus Christ.

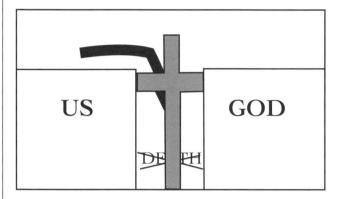

Finally, draw an arrow showing us crossing to the other side. Explain that we are able to do this when we admit to God that we need his forgiveness and we desire to follow him.

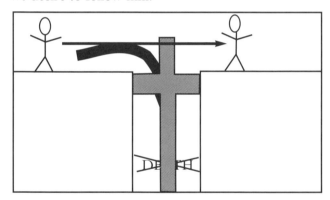

Coming to God is as Easy as ABC :

◆ **Admit** that you are not living the kind of life God wants for you, and that you want to change. "All have sinned and fall short of the glory of God" (Romans 3:23).

◆ **Believe** Jesus is God's Son, and he is the only way to salvation. "Jesus said to him, 'I am the way, and the truth, and the life. No one comes to the Father except through Me'" (John 14:6).

◆ **Confess** what you have done wrong, and that you need God in your life, and confess to another person that you have made a decision to follow him. "If you confess with your lips that Jesus is Lord and believe in your heart that God raised him from the dead, you will be saved" (Romans 10:9).

The Fishing illustration: This illustration is good to use with nominal believers. We can study the science of fishing, spend lots of time at the lake, learn all about lures and bait. But we are not actually fishing until we drop a line into the water. Likewise, going to church and volunteering our time is not enough to make us Christians; we must have a personal relationship with Christ and receive forgiveness.

3. Why do people need the Church?

It is important to answer this question, because many people claim that they do not need organized religion to be faithful. They might say something such as, "Churches are full of hypocrites!" Well, of course they are—hypocrites, liars, drug addicts, and sinners of every kind. Jesus built the church specifically for them! That excuse is a cop out. There are some very specific reasons that every believer needs the church. Here are the primary reasons:

◆ We are commanded to meet together and encourage one another. Hebrews 10:24-25 says this: "And let us consider how to provoke one another to love and good deeds, not neglecting to meet together, as is the habit of some, but encouraging one another." Christianity was made to be lived out in community. The disciples were Jesus' community. We need one, too.
◆ Spiritual growth and maturity happen most effectively in community. When believers gather together in worship, fellowship, discipleship, and service, they encourage one another, hold one another accountable for Christian behavior, and support one another in tough times.
◆ Together we can accomplish much more than we can on our own. Each believer is given spiritual gifts with which we are called to serve others and glorify God. Every believer's gifts are needed. The apostle Paul used the analogy of the "body of Christ" in 1 Corinthians 12 to illustrate how the body functions much less effectively when some of its parts are not contributing. Jesus is counting on us!

Look for an Opportunity

When it comes to sharing your faith with others, how do you know when the time is right? First and foremost, be sensitive to the prompting of the Holy Spirit. Be aware of feeling compelled to talk to someone about your faith—most likely this is a "nudging" from the Holy Spirit. Pay attention, and then be willing. Second, be sensitive to the situation. Do you have the person's undivided attention, or are you in a group which might make the person uncomfortable or unreceptive? If the time is right, then you must decide how to approach the subject.

One approach is to be direct. Keep in mind that being direct does not mean being aggressive. It just means being straightforward. If the person asks a question about God or about your faith, he or she is signaling that the door is open to direct conversation. If the person is despairing about how he'll get through a difficult time, you might try a direct approach, such as saying, "My faith in Jesus helps me through times like these. He will help you too, if you'll let him…" The other person will let you know pretty quickly whether or not he or she is interested in talking about matters of faith. If the person rejects your approach, don't take it personally—some people simply don't respond well to the direct approach.

In their book *Becoming a Contagious Christian*, Bill Hybels and Mark Mittleberg suggest a more subtle method called *bridging (GrandRapids: Zondervan, 1994, p. 141)*. This is done in the midst of a non-spiritual conversation by taking some element of the discussion topic and using it to turn the conversation toward God, the church, or faith. For instance, if you are talking to someone about your weekend, you could talk about how much fun you had at the Christian concert you attended on Friday night, and how much the music fed you spiritually. Or, during difficult circumstances in your life, you could respond to others' inquiries about how you are doing by sharing how the prayers and support of your Christian friends have encouraged you. In a conversation about a professional football game, you might bring up how one of the players attributes his success to his faith in God.

However you begin a spiritual conversation with an unbeliever, you must convey your belief that your relationship with Jesus has changed your life for the better and the same can be true for the unbeliever you are addressing. That, in reality, is the whole truth of why we share our faith. We know the difference Jesus has made in our lives, and we want others to have that, too. Even if you stumble as you tell the gospel message, and even if the person does not accept Jesus, you can feel good because you were faithful to Christ's call to be his ambassador, witness, and disciple.

Remember, all you have to do is be willing to share what you know and what you have experienced. The power to convert a non-believer to Christianity belongs to the Holy Spirit, and the results are up to God. Sharing our faith with other believers is important, too. By doing so, we encourage one another and strengthen one another's faith, which may help to prepare us to witness to others.

Biblical Foundation

As you review each Scripture passage, underline or circle key words or phrases. Think about the implications of each passage for your life, noting your insights in the space provided. Answer the questions that follow.

God…wants all people to be saved and to come to a knowledge of the truth. (1 Timothy 2:4 NIV)

So [Jesus] told them this parable: "Which one of you, having a hundred sheep and losing one of them, does not leave the ninety-nine in the wilderness and go after the one that is lost until he finds it? When he has found it, he lays it on his shoulders and rejoices. And when he comes home, he calls together his friends and neighbors, saying to them, 'Rejoice with me, for I have found my sheep that was lost.' Just so, I tell you, there will be more joy in heaven over one

sinner who repents than over ninety-nine righteous persons who need no repentance." (Luke 15:3-7, 10)

"The Son of Man came to seek out and to save the lost." (Luke 19:10)

"As the Father has sent me, so I send you." (John 20:21b)

"You will receive power when the Holy Spirit has come upon you; and you will be my witnesses in Jerusalem, in all Judea and Samaria, and to the ends of the earth." (Acts 1:8)

God… reconciled us to himself through Christ, and has given us the ministry of reconciliation; that is, in Christ God was reconciling the world to himself, not counting their trespasses against them, and entrusting the message of reconciliation to us. So we are ambassadors for Christ, since God is making his appeal through us. (2 Corinthians 5:18-20a)

How can people call for help if they don't know who to trust? And how can they know who to trust if they haven't heard of the One who can be trusted? And how can they hear if nobody tells them?" (Romans 10:14, Msg.)

In your hearts set apart Christ as Lord. Always be prepared to give an answer to everyone who asks you to give the reason for the hope that you have. But do this with gentleness and respect, keeping a clear conscience, so that those who speak maliciously against your good behavior in Christ may be ashamed of their slander. (1 Peter 3:15-16 NIV)

I pray that you may be active in sharing your faith, so that you will have a full understanding of every good thing we have in Christ. (Philemon 6 NIV)

Reflection Questions

1. What was Christ's mission here on earth?

2. Who was Jesus talking about when he spoke about the "lost"?

3. Who are the "lost" in today's world, and where can they be found?

4. Why should we care about the "lost"? Why are we called to share our faith?

5. Where are we to share our faith?

6. How are we to share our faith?

7. What is the result in our own lives of sharing our faith?

 # HEART

Taking It to Heart

1. Describe your past experiences with sharing your faith. What types of responses have you received? If you have never shared your faith with an unbeliever, what fears are holding you back? How can you overcome them?

2. What are the risks of sharing your faith?

3. What might the rewards be?

4. Which style of evangelism best fits you? Why?

5. In the space below, or on a separate sheet of paper, write an outline of your own personal testimony. Include three sections: 1) what your life was like before you knew Christ, or your experience growing up in a Christian home; 2) your conversion experience, or how you came to embrace the faith of your parents; and 3) what your life has been like since you accepted Christ and how you have changed and continue to grow.

   1.

   2.

   3.

Heart to Heart

1. As a group, develop a two- to three-sentence summary of the video presentation.

2. Discuss the Scripture readings from this week's reading. How did God speak to you through these passages?

3. Pair up with one or two members of your small group and take turns sharing your personal testimonies.

4. Discuss how you might bridge a conversation on the following topics to a discussion about faith:

   Nature or the weather

   Sports

   An episode of a popular television show

   Your vacation

5. Discuss different methods of explaining the gospel. Which ones seem most comfortable for you and why?

 **HANDS**

Action Plan

1. With your accountability partner(s), briefly share your experience in affirming the gifts of two individuals the previous week.

2. Prepare to share your testimony with two fellow believers during the coming week. Plan to use your outline, if necessary (see #5 in Taking It to Heart). You can explain to them that you are trying to get comfortable sharing your story. Try to get your testimony down to five minutes or less. After you have shared your testimony, describe the experiences below.

Person One:

Person Two:

3. Now select a person in your life (an existing relationship) who is not a believer and to whom you would like to witness. Pray for this person and for yourself. Make time to meet with this person and begin a spiritual conversation. If the person seems open to listening, share your testimony and explain the gospel message. Complete the following "action plan," and then briefly share with your accountability partner(s). You'll have an opportunity to share your experience with your partner(s) next week.

What is the person's name?

When and where will you meet with him or her?

Which gospel illustration(s) will you use?

After your meeting, describe the experience below:

BEING SALT AND LIGHT
Transforming a Community

SESSION 6

Materials Needed:

◆ nametags
◆ pens or pencils
◆ TV and DVD player

For opening activity:
◆ "Lifeboat" instruction sheet for each group (see DVD)
◆ enough small paper "ballots" for each participant

Room Set-up:

◆ Arrange pre-assigned groups around tables so that members are facing one another.
◆ Place TV and DVD player so that all can see (participants may need to turn their chairs around to view video).

Timing:

This outline is designed to cover a ninety-minute session. If you prefer to fit this into a sixty-minute format, we suggest deleting the Opening Activity and reducing the Heart to Heart Small Group Discussion to thirty minutes and the Hands Action Plan to ten minutes. If you prefer a two-hour format, include a fifteen-minute break after the Video Presentation Discussion, and add fifteen minutes to the Heart to Heart Small Group Discussion.

Opening Prayer and Welcome
(5 minutes)

Welcome participants to *Leadership from the Heart*, Session 6. The purpose of this session is to understand that we are Christ's body, his physical representation to others. As such, he is relying on us to serve and care for those in need, just as he did during his time on earth.

Opening Activity
(10 minutes)

*Do not share the purpose of this activity with participants until after the activity is completed. Doing so will undermine the process of self-discovery, which is important for adult learning.

The purpose of this activity is to help participants realize the impact when someone is either "left out" or not included. This activity should provoke feelings of discomfort. Participants are left to think of the implications for people who feel excluded from our churches. Do not be surprised if, in a desire to "save" everyone, groups deviate from the activity's instructions.

Give each group a copy of the Lifeboat instruction sheet and enough small sheets of paper "ballots" for every group member. As outlined in the instructions, each group member will have thirty seconds to present his or her case to the group. After all have finished, the group will vote by secret ballot which member should be voted out of the lifeboat. Votes should be read aloud, and the person voted out of the lifeboat should either physically leave the table or stand with his or her back to everyone else. Allow five minutes for them to complete the assignment.

Bring the full group back together to debrief the activity.

Use the following questions to generate a short discussion (allow five minutes for this):

◆ How did you feel having to plead to stay in the lifeboat?
◆ How did it feel to vote someone out of the boat?
◆ How might we relate these feelings to those experienced by people who, for one reason or another, feel excluded from our church?

Video Presentation

Jonathan Bell (Approx. 9 minutes)

Play the video segment for Session 6.

Full Group Video Discussion

(5 minutes)

Facilitate a full group discussion based on the video presentation using the questions that follow. Don't be nervous if no one responds immediately. If there is a pause and you do not fill in the silence, someone eventually will speak up! After someone responds, ask for other comments. After one or two comments, go on to the next question, and so forth. Try to keep this initial discussion brief and to the point. Inform the participants that more in-depth discussion will follow in their small groups.

1. Sometimes churches do become more like "country clubs" than "life-saving" stations. How or why does that happen, and what can we do to prevent it?
2. The speaker stated that when we serve and care for those suffering, in need, or living without hope, the love of God becomes real in the world—"on Earth as it is in Heaven." How is that true?
3. What other insights did you glean from this video?

Bring the group back to this key point:

Mission work—serving and caring for people in need—is not the sole responsibility of a ministry area within our church. It is the responsibility of each of us. We make the love of God a tangible reality when we love and serve the "least of these."

Heart to Heart Small Group Discussions

(40 minutes)

Each small group guide should start the discussion by reminding group members that the discussion questions are not designed to have "right" or "wrong" answers. They are meant to encourage group members to share their own insights and experiences, as well as what they've learned, so that members of the group can learn from one another. Everyone has something to offer! The guide should encourage each person to participate, and should keep any one individual from dominating the discussion. Refer to the Tips for Small Group Guides in this *Leader's Guide* (page 8) for pointers on group facilitation.

Begin by asking the group to summarize the video presentation. Groups should try to get that message into a few short sentences.

Ask group members which passage(s) from this week's Scripture spoke to them and why.

Continue the discussion using the Heart to Heart questions on page 78.

Hands Action Plan

(15 minutes)

Small group guides should direct group members to get with their accountability partner(s) and proceed with the Hands portion of the session on page 78.

First, they each take one minute reporting their progress on last week's action plan. What did and did not happen as they had hoped?

Next, they take six to eight minutes developing their action plans for this week.

Finally, each one shares his or her action plan for the upcoming week.

Closing Circle Prayer

(5 minutes)

Small group guides should bring the accountability partners of the small groups back together for joys and concerns and a closing prayer. Ask the participants to keep their comments brief, encouraging them to share detailed prayer requests outside of class time—either in person, on the phone, or via e-mail.

We encourage you to use a circle prayer format to close the small group time. The ability to lead a group in prayer is essential in

Christian leadership, but many people are not comfortable praying aloud. Circle prayers are useful in helping people become comfortable praying in a group. Remind the participants that their words do not have to be elaborate—just from the heart!

Have members stand, if they are able, holding hands around the table. Ask each person to speak one sentence in prayer, with the small group guide opening and closing the prayer.

CHAPTER 6

BEING SALT AND LIGHT
Transforming a Community

"You are the salt of the earth; but if salt has lost its taste, how can its saltiness be restored? It is no longer good for anything, but is thrown out and trampled under foot. You are the light of the world.... No one after lighting a lamp puts it under the bushel basket, but on the lampstand, and it gives light to all in the house. In the same way, let your light shine before others, so that they may see your good works and give glory to your Father in heaven."

(Matthew 5:13-14a, 15-16)

 HEAD

Key Insights

◆ We are called not only to believe and conduct our lives according to our faith, but also to *do* something in response—to take action.

◆ We can influence our communities and culture by "being Christ" for those who are hurting, in need, or oppressed.

Understanding the Concept

Called to Be Salt and Light

Jesus told us we are to be salt and light to the world. What did he mean, and why did he use those terms? In Christ's time, salt served two purposes. It was a preservative, preventing decay, and it provided seasoning for taste. Lamps also had more than one purpose. They were used to illuminate the darkness and to provide warmth and safety. Both salt and light were used to change things for the better. By telling us that we are to be salt and light to the world, Jesus was saying that we are to be positive influences in the world.

The Old Testament tells the story of how God repeatedly sought to redeem the world, first calling Abraham to follow him, then sending Moses to deliver his people from bondage, and then directing the prophets to lead his people back to him. The

New Testament continues the story, this time with God's ultimate personal sacrifice for the redemption of his people through the death and resurrection of his own Son, Jesus. God wants all people to be redeemed. Jesus told us to be salt and light so that others may see our good works and give praise to God (Matthew 5:16)—in other words, so that they will *believe and follow* him.

People want desperately to believe in something—or *Someone*—that gives life, purpose, and meaning, yet the world promotes an attitude of trusting only what can be seen, touched, or experienced. The truth of the gospel becomes interesting to non-believers only after they witness the credibility of Christians and understand that the gospel has relevance to their own lives. The most effective way to draw people to Christ, then, is not through being "more religious," but through being "more connected." We need to spend less time focusing on what's wrong with the world and more time making things better by demonstrating God's love.

Some Christians actually defeat their own purpose by preaching that the world is lost and all non-Christians are damned. That aggressive approach usually does not draw people in but, instead, creates hostility and alienation between churches and communities. When Christ met the Samaritan woman at the well, he did not condemn her for marrying and divorcing five times, or for living with a man she was not married to then.

Instead, he showed kindness and compassion, offering to give her "living water" so she would never go thirsty again (see John 4:7-10). Likewise, we must *live* what we preach—we must be the Body of Christ, serving others in tangible ways. Adam Hamilton, senior pastor of Church of the Resurrection in Leawood, Kansas, often says that when Christ was here on earth, he went from place to place ministering one-on-one to the needs of the people he met. Christ is no longer here on earth in physical form; instead, we are his body, called to be his hands and his voice in a broken world.

If our faith is to have any impact whatsoever on our culture, it must be put into action. What James wrote in New Testament times is still true today: "Faith without works is…dead" (James 2:26). Jesus prayed for the disciples and for all believers who would come after them, not that they would be taken out of the world but that they might be sent into the world. He explained why with these words: "So that the world may know that you have sent me and have loved them even as you have loved me" (John 17:23).

You see, the gospel *always* brings social responsibility. Jesus called it loving our neighbor. The Greek word for love used in Matthew 22:39, where we are told to love our neighbor as ourselves, is *agape*, which means to "love in a social or moral sense." In other words, it refers more to loving actions than to loving feelings. Think about the New Testament church and how it exploded across the world. This happened not only because the believers were passionately committed to Jesus Christ and to proclaiming the gospel, but also because they lived lives of such active love and selflessness that the communities they lived in could not help but notice.

Reluctant to "Get Involved"

Regrettably, we Christians today often hesitate to "get involved" in helping those outside the church. Some of us try to isolate ourselves as much as possible from negative cultural influences and even non-believers in an attempt to stay "pure." We need to keep in mind, however, that salt preserves only what it touches. Instead of being shocked by our culture and isolating ourselves, we must infiltrate our culture to prevent cultural decay and serve as seasoning for our communities, resulting in positive change.

Others of us think that we cannot possibly have an impact. After all, as Robert Lewis points out in *The Church of Irresistible Influence*, there are more than 170 million non-believers in America alone, making our country the third largest mission field in the world (Grand Rapids: Zondervan, 2001, p. 23). We ask ourselves, "What difference can *I* make?" Nineteenth century author and minister Edward Everett Hale said, "I am only one but I am still one. I cannot do everything, but I can still do something" (*Life's Interruptions, God's Opportunities: Lessons from the Good Samaritan* [Nashville: J. Countryman, 2002] p. 75). Let me tell you a story of one person's impact.

A few years ago, I participated in a Bible study with eighteen other people. One of them was a woman named Mina. She shared during one session that she knows what it is like to be poor and to have needs go unmet. Now that she is able, she feels compelled to give something back. Every winter she buys a bag full of inexpensive gloves. As she drives to work through a poor part of town, she looks for homeless people on the side of the street, stops her car, rolls down the window, and tosses them a pair of gloves with a blessing. The class laughed about these "drive-by glovings," but all of us in that group were convicted by our own failure to do something—anything—for people in need.

Still others of us are afraid we will not know what to say when we are face-to-face with someone in need. We forget that what they really need is not our eloquence but simply our expression of love and care. Martin Luther King, Jr. said, "Anybody can serve. You don't have to have a college degree to serve. You don't have to make your subject and verb agree to serve. You don't have to know Einstein's theory of relativity to serve. All you need is a heart full of grace, a soul formed in love" (*The Drum Major Instinct*, sermon preached by Martin Luther King Jr. at Ebenezer Baptist Church, Atlanta, Georgia, February 4, 1968). Perhaps the most common excuse we give, however, is time. We are too busy, we say. We avoid personal involvement and prefer to simply write a check, thinking we have done our part. Monetary support for missions is a worthy investment and critical for the work to continue, both within our country and throughout the world. However, the blessings for both the server and the served are much richer when we let our love wear "work clothes."

In his book *Life's Interruptions, God's Opportunities: Lessons from the Good Samaritan*, Larry Jones writes these convicting words:

> We stay conveniently separated from the poor…enjoying all the accoutrements that accompany the good life we've worked so hard to achieve. These material things aren't necessarily wrong, but we will never impress the poor with our homes, boats, cars, or Rolex watches. We can only impress them with our love. And to love them, you have to rub shoulders with poor people ([Nashville: J. Countryman, 2002] p. 37).

Unfortunately, many churches also stay conveniently separated from the poor, focusing only on themselves. Two primary concerns of inward-focused churches are meeting the needs of church members and striving for dynamic growth in numbers—neither of which does anything to help or transform the lives of those outside the church. Churches that want to be "salt and light" must go beyond themselves to make a difference in the community.

Both as individuals and as the church, we must take the time to be *personally* involved in missions. We must let go of our excuses and accept Christ's call to be "salt and light." When we do, our actions will begin to draw people to Christ. Many people who will not respond to the spoken gospel will respond when they see and experience it firsthand. People who never have been interested in Christianity—and even may have been hostile toward it—will actually thirst for the gospel as we consistently prove the love of Christ in tangible ways. Remember, a lamp gives light not from a distance, but as it moves *through* the darkness, illuminating dark corners of fear with the warmth of love and hope.

Ready to Take Action

When we're ready to take action, where do we begin? John Wesley developed a rule that he lived by: "Do all the good you can, by all the means you can, in all the ways you can, in all the places you can, to all the people you can, as long as ever you can" (*Letters of John Wesley*, George Eayrs, ed. [London, New York: Hodder & Stoughton, 1915] p. 423, footnote). The good we do does not have to be newsworthy or spectacular. Often it is the small things we do that are the most loving—providing a pair of gloves or a warm meal or a loving smile. As Mother Teresa said, "We do no great things, only small things with great love" (*In the Silence of the Heart*, Kathryn Spink, ed. [London, SPCK Publishers, 1983]).

When love is our motivation, our acts of service have a far greater impact than we might imagine. I think again of Mina and her influence on the individuals in our Bible study group. During one class session, she suggested that we participate as a group in the church's food drive, with each person bringing a non-perishable food item to class each week. Every week, Mina brought her food item and placed it on the table in front of her as a reminder to others. This attitude of compassion-moved-to-action became infectious. Our class adopted a family for Christmas, served together at a local mission opportunity, collected money for a church in an underprivileged section of town, and made sack lunches for the homeless. Not only did Mina have an impact on the lives of the people she served individually, but she also made a significant impact on each person in that Bible study, serving as an example to us all and reminding us of Christ's call to love our neighbor.

There are countless ways you can begin to take action. Like Mina, you can take action on your own, and you can get involved in serving the hungry, clothing the poor, or helping the needy through your church or various community agencies. You can serve in ongoing church outreach ministries, or you can participate in one-time events where all you are required to do is show up on a Saturday morning and give half a day in service to others. You can volunteer to help with Habitat for Humanity, building homes for people in need, or participate in a church or community-sponsored Angel Tree program, buying and delivering Christmas gifts to a child who otherwise would have none. Another way to get involved is to take part in a mission trip. Some mission trips take place close to home and are less expensive to participate in, while others involve overseas travel and require a monetary investment to cover your travel expenses and time.

However you choose to serve, remember that you set the example as a leader in the church. So we must model the importance of involvement in missions for those we lead. You have a responsibility to model the importance of involvement in missions for those you lead, affirming this kind of effort as spiritual service to God. Jonathan Bell, Director of Missions at Church of the Resurrection, says that leaders should do three things in regards to missions:

◆ REMEMBER the biblical story of what God has been doing since the twelfth chapter of Genesis to redeem the world, as well as what that story tells us about God's mission and the purpose of the church. Involvement in missions is how we prove God's love for people in tangible ways, making them thirst for the redemption found in the gospel.

◆ PRAY for God to guide your heart in his way and toward his will, for the courage to follow where God is leading, and for the patience to do what it takes to involve others.

◆ INVOLVE OTHERS by doing what it takes to create opportunities for others to serve. As leaders, this means taking the initiative to bring missions opportunities to the groups we lead, encouraging them to take part, making it easy for them to get involved, and always reminding them of the purpose.

The story is told of a church in Poland that was bombed during World War II. A large statue of Christ in front of the church was hit during one of the bombings, and the hands were blown off. The statue was never restored. Today the hands are still missing. At the foot of the statue, however, someone

inscribed these words: "Christ has no hands but yours." The question we must ask ourselves and pose to those we lead is this: How can Christ use my (or your) hands today?

Biblical Foundation

As you review each Scripture passage, underline or circle key words or phrases. Think about the implications of each passage for your life, noting your insights in the space provided. Answer the questions that follow.

One of the scribes came near and heard them disputing with one another, and seeing that he had answered them well, he asked him, "Which commandment is the first of all?" Jesus answered, "The first is, 'Hear, O Israel! The Lord our God, the Lord is one; shall love the Lord your God with all your heart, and with all your soul, and with all your mind, and with all your strength.' And the second is this, 'You shall love your neighbor as yourself.' There is no other commandment greater than these." (Mark 12:28-31)

When [Jesus] came to Nazareth, where he had been brought up, he went to the synagogue on the Sabbath day, as was his custom. He stood up to read, and the scroll of the prophet Isaiah was given to him. He unrolled the scroll and found the place where it was written, "The Spirit of the Lord is upon me, because he has anointed me to bring good news to the poor. He has sent me to proclaim release to the captives, and recovery of sight to the blind, and to let the oppressed go free, to proclaim the year of the Lord's favor." And he rolled up the scroll, gave it back to the attendant, and sat down. The eyes of all in the synagogue were fixed on him. Then he began to say to them, "Today this Scripture has been fulfilled in your hearing." (Luke 4:16-21)

Jesus went about all the cities and villages, teaching in their synagogues, and proclaiming the good news of the kingdom, and curing every disease and every sickness. When he saw the crowds, he had compassion for them, because they were harassed and helpless, like sheep without a shepherd. Then he said to his disciples, "The harvest is plentiful but the laborers are few; therefore ask the Lord of the harvest to send out laborers into his harvest." (Matthew 9:35-38)

Whoever is kind to the poor lends to the Lord, and will be repaid in full. (Proverbs 19:17)

Whoever has two coats is to share with anyone who has none; and whoever has food must do likewise. (Luke 3:11)

"Then the king will say to those at his right hand, 'Come, you that are blessed by my Father; inherit the kingdom prepared for you from the foundation of the world; for I was hungry and you gave me food, I was thirsty and you gave me something to drink, I was a stranger and you welcomed me, I was naked and you gave me clothing, I was sick and you took care of me, I was in prison and you visited me.' Then the righteous will answer him, 'Lord, when was it that we saw you hungry and gave you food, or thirsty and gave you something to drink? And when was it that we saw you a stranger and welcomed you, or naked and gave you clothing? And when was it that we saw you sick or in prison and visited you?' The king will answer them, 'Truly I tell you, just as you did it to one of the least of these who are members of my family, you did it to me.'"
(Matthew 25:34-40)

Just then a lawyer stood up to test Jesus. "Teacher," he said, "what must I do to inherit eternal life?" He said to him, "What is written in the Law? What do you read there?" He answered, "'You shall love the Lord your God with all your heart, and with all your soul, and with all your strength, and with all your mind,' and 'your neighbor as yourself.'" And he said to him, "You have given the right answer; do this, and you will live." But wanting to justify himself, he asked Jesus, "And who is my neighbor?" Jesus replied, "A man was going down from Jerusalem to Jericho, and fell

into the hands of robbers, who stripped him, beat him, and went away, leaving him half dead. Now by chance a priest was going down that road; and when he saw him, he passed by on the other side. So likewise a Levite, when he came to the place and saw him, passed by on the other side. But a Samaritan while traveling came near him; and when he saw him, he was moved with pity. He went to him and bandaged his wounds, having poured oil and wine on them. Then he put him on his own animal, brought him to an inn, and took care of him. The next day he took out two denarii, gave them to the innkeeper, and said, 'Take care of him; and when I come back, I will repay you whatever more you spend.' Which of these three, do you think, was a neighbor to the man who fell into the hands of the robbers?" He said, "The one who showed him mercy." Jesus said to him, "Go and do likewise." (Luke 10: 25-37)

What good is it, my brothers and sisters, if a person claims to have faith but has no deeds? Can such a faith save him or her? Suppose a brother or sister is without clothes and daily food. If one of you says to him, "Go, I wish you well; keep warm and well fed," but does nothing about his physical needs, what good is it? In the same way, faith by itself, if it is not accompanied by action, is dead.
(James 2:14-17 NIV)

They devoted themselves to the apostles' teaching and fellowship, to the breaking of bread and the prayers. Awe came upon everyone, because many wonders and signs were being done by the apostles. All who believed were together and had all things in common; they would sell their possessions and goods and distribute the proceeds to all, as any had need. Day by day they spent much time together in the temple, they broke bread at home and ate their food with glad and generous hearts, praising God and having the goodwill of all the people. And day by day the Lord added to their number those who were being saved. (Acts 2:42-47)

How does God's love abide in anyone who has the world's good and sees a brother or sister in need and yet refuses to help? Little children, let us love, not in word or speech, but in truth and action. (1 John 3:17-18)

Be wise in the way you act toward outsiders; make the most of every opportunity. Let your conversation be always full of grace, seasoned with salt, so that you may know how to answer everyone. (Colossians 4:5-6 NIV)

For so the Lord has commanded us, saying, "I have set you to be a light for the Gentiles, so that you may bring salvation to the end of the earth." (Acts 13:47)

Reflection Questions

1. What do you think Jesus meant when he said, "Love your neighbor as yourself"?

2. Read 1 John 3:18. How do we love with actions and in truth?

3. Read Matthew 25:34-40. How might we act differently if we think about every action we take—or do not take—being done—or not done—to Jesus?

4. What is the purpose of being salt and light to the world?

 **HEART**

Taking It to Heart

1. What does being "salt and light" for the world mean to you personally?

2 If you always remembered that *everything* you do has an influence on non-believers, how would that change your behavior?

3. How does the thought of being "Christ's hands" in the world make you feel?

4. Have you ever participated in a missions or outreach activity? If so, describe the experience and how it made you feel. If not, what concerns or fears have prevented you from doing so?

Heart to Heart

1. As a group, develop a two- to three-sentence summary of the video presentation.

2. Discuss the Scripture passages from this week's reading. What does it mean to be "salt and light" in the world?

3. Share your thoughts and feelings about being "Christ's hands" in the world.

4. When Jesus said we are to love our neighbors as ourselves, he was not referring to a feeling of love, but an action of love. He said that this is the second most important commandment. If we take this to heart, how will it influence our lives?

5. Discuss your mission or outreach experiences. We have said that the person serving also receives blessings by their actions. How has this been true in your experience?

 **HANDS**

Action Plan

1. With your accountability partner(s), briefly share your experience witnessing to an unbeliever during the previous week.

2. Over the next week, research missions opportunities within the church as well as through community agencies. How can you get involved as an individual? What opportunities exist for groups (e.g., church groups, friends, family) to get involved? Be prepared to share what you discover with your accountability partner(s) next week. If you are currently involved in a study or fellowship group, either as a leader or a participant, suggest to the group that you do a missions project together sometime. If you are not involved in a group, consider how you might get your friends or family involved in a project.

   How will you bring up the topic?

   What opportunities will you suggest?

   When would this project take place?

3. Briefly share your ideas with your accountability partner(s).

A CITY ON A HILL
Renewing the Church

SESSION 7

Materials Needed:

◆ nametags
◆ pens or pencils
◆ TV and DVD player

For opening activity:
◆ The activity can be done in groups as small as five and as large as twenty, though eight to ten participants is an optimal size. You will need one activity facilitator per group.
◆ a paper bag with up to ten objects that are soft and can be caught when thrown across a circle

Room Set-up:

◆ Arrange pre-assigned groups around tables so that members are facing one another.
◆ Place TV and DVD player so that all can see (participants may need to turn their chairs around to view video).

Timing:

This outline is designed to cover a ninety-minute session. If you prefer to fit this into a sixty-minute format, we suggest deleting the Opening Activity and reducing the Heart to Heart Small Group Discussion to thirty minutes and the Hands Action Plan to ten minutes. If you prefer a two-hour format, include a fifteen-minute break after the Video Presentation Discussion, and add fifteen minutes to the Heart to Heart Small Group Discussion.

Opening Prayer and Welcome

(5 minutes)

Welcome participants to *Leadership from the Heart*, Session 7. The purpose of this session is to gain an understanding that, like so many other things in life, our churches are constantly in need of renewal. As leaders, we are called to be forces for positive change, keeping our faith alive.

Opening Activity

(10 minutes)

Do not share the purpose of this activity with participants until after the activity is completed. Doing so will undermine the process of self-discovery, which is important for adult learning.

The purpose of this activity is to help participants realize the discomfort we often feel when introduced to change or something unfamiliar to us.

Split the full group into smaller circles of eight to ten people in an open area of the room. (The activity can be done in groups as small as five or as large as twenty.) Have a facilitator stand in each circle with the bag of soft objects. The facilitator will begin by throwing one object to someone across the circle. The facilitator will instruct that person to do the same, saying the name of the person (the catcher) out loud as he or she tosses the item. Repeat this until everyone in the circle has had an opportunity to catch the object once, and only once. Give the object back to the facilitator and repeat the same thing, making sure to go in exactly the same order as the first time. Once the pattern is well-established—in other words, the group is comfortable throwing the object in the exact same order every time—take a second item out of the bag. Throw the first object in the established pattern; then throw the second object to another person. Add a third to still another person. Stop the game. Now the facilitator will ask participants to reverse the pattern, throwing the objects in reverse order, starting

wherever they left off, and this time having the catchers call out the name of the person throwing the object. The facilitator should keep adding objects until chaos ensues. Allow six to seven minutes for the game.

Bring the full group back together. Use the following questions to generate a short discussion (allow four minutes for this):

1. How did you feel at the beginning of the game when only one object was being thrown?
2. Contrast this with how you felt at the end of the game.
3. How might the feelings you experienced by the end of the game compare with those of people experiencing our church for the first time?

Video Presentation

Adam Hamilton (Approx. 9 minutes)

Play the video segment for Session 7.

Full Group Video Discussion

(5 minutes)

Facilitate a full group discussion based on the video presentation using the questions that follow. Don't be nervous if no one responds immediately. If there is a pause and you do not fill in the silence, someone eventually will speak up! After someone responds, ask for other comments. After one or two comments, go on to the next question, and so forth. Try to keep this initial discussion brief and to the point. Inform the participants that more in-depth discussion will follow in their small groups.

1. The speaker quoted a phrase that arose during the Protestant Reformation: "The Church that is reformed is always reforming." What does that mean for us?
2. What are your thoughts when you consider that the Old Testament as a history of God's people needing continuous renewal and reformation, and that Jesus himself started a renewal movement?

3. What other insights did you glean from this video?

Bring the group back to this key point:
Our human nature is to become complacent, losing that passion we once had. For that reason, the church is continually reforming. We have a long history of cyclical renewal, and that cycle continues with us today.

Heart to Heart Small Group Discussions

(40 minutes)

Each small group guide should start the discussion by reminding group members that the discussion questions are not designed to have "right" or "wrong" answers. They are meant to encourage group members to share their own insights and experiences, as well as what they've learned, so that members of the group can learn from one another. Everyone has something to offer! The guide should encourage each person to participate, and should keep any one individual from dominating the discussion. Refer to the Tips for Small group Guides in this *Leader's Guide* (page 8) for pointers on group facilitation.

Begin by asking the group to summarize the video presentation. Groups should try to get that message into a few short sentences.

Ask group members which passage(s) from this week's Scripture spoke to them and why.

Continue the discussion using the Heart to Heart questions on page 87.

Hands Action Plan

(15 minutes)

Small group guides should direct group members to get with their accountability partner(s) and proceed with the Hands portion of the session on page 87.

First, they each take one minute reporting their progress on last week's action plan. What did and did not happen as they had hoped?

Next, they take six to eight minutes developing their action plans for this week.

Finally, each one shares his or her action plan for the upcoming week.

Closing Circle Prayer

(5 minutes)

Small group guides should bring the accountability partners of the small groups back together for joys and concerns and a closing prayer. Ask the participants to keep their comments brief, encouraging them to share detailed prayer requests outside of class time— either in person, on the phone, or via e-mail.

We encourage you to use a circle prayer format to close the small group time. The ability to lead a group in prayer is essential in Christian leadership, but many people are not comfortable praying aloud. Circle prayers are useful in helping people become comfortable praying in a group. Remind the participants that their words do not have to be elaborate— just from the heart!

Have members stand, if they are able, holding hands around the table. Ask each person to speak one sentence in prayer, with the small group guide opening and closing the prayer.

A CITY ON A HILL
Renewing the Church

CHAPTER 7

"You are the light of the world. A city built on a hill cannot be hid. No one after lighting a lamp puts it under the bushel basket, but on the lampstand, and it gives light to all in the house. In the same way, let your light shine before others, so that they may see your good works and give glory to your Father in heaven." (Matthew 5:14-16)

 HEAD

Key Insights

◆ There are a variety of Christian denominations or church organizations, yet we are called to be one body—diverse yet unified.

◆ Many church organizations are experiencing crises in terms of trust, relevance, and growth.

◆ To maintain vitality, the church needs constant renewal.

◆ As leaders, Christ expects us to serve as agents of positive change, making his church attractive to the outside world.

Understanding the Concept

A couple of years ago, my dentist recommended I buy one of those fancy "sonic" toothbrushes. It was pretty expensive, but he assured me it would be worth it because it would clean much more effectively than a manual toothbrush. It did—for about six days. I noticed that it began to move a little more slowly, and then it sputtered, and finally, it ran out of power altogether. I had forgotten to recharge its battery! That night I put the toothbrush into its charger, and voila! Its power was renewed, and once again it cleaned my teeth effectively.

The church, like my electric toothbrush, needs regular recharging to maintain its effectiveness. Throughout history, there have been repeated cycles of religious renewal. The Old Testament is replete with stories of this cycle. The people are close to God for a while, and then they wander; then there are calls for renewal and rededication to their faith, which lead them back to a close relationship with God. In a sense, the church is always reforming, always seeking renewal. Many of our denominations formed out of renewal or reform movements.

Recently there have been calls for renewal in nearly every church organization in our country. Our churches are struggling. Why? The answer is different for each group, but there is one problem they have in common: Their ability to influence today's culture is growing weaker as generations of people lose trust in organized religion, find its message to be irrelevant, or simply do not feel any "connection" with a local church. In this chapter, we will examine a few of the issues causing this, as well as what we can do as leaders to bring about change. Before we examine those issues, let's define renewal. According to Webster's New World Dictionary, to renew means "to make new or fresh again; to reestablish; revive" ([New York: Warner Books, 1984]. When we seek to bring renewal to our churches, we strive to make them fresh, to bring new life to them, to reestablish their vibrancy and vitality.

As we review the issues that have led to calls for renewal, consider how they apply to the church as a whole, your denomination, your local congregation, and your leadership.

Gaining Trust

In earlier chapters, we talked about the need for trust in any leader-follower relationship. Followers need to know they can count on those people who lead the way. They want leaders who give them something to believe in, and who then model that in their own lives. They watch to see if their leaders are "walking the walk."

That is also how people decide whether or not they can trust an organization. They look to see if the organization is living up to its espoused values. Christian churches receive particularly close scrutiny. When we consider Jesus' teachings, we find one value he stood for above all others: love. He said, "By this everyone will know that you are my disciples, if you have love for one another" (John 13:35). Notice that Jesus did *not* say, "If you all baptize by the same method, follow the same procedure for observing Holy Communion, and all pray the same words, people will know you are my disciples." Instead, his words were, "…if you have *love* for one another."

Yet we, as churches, sometimes do not show love towards one another. Whether we're talking about a scandal occurring in another denomination (as if it could never happen in *our* church!), or looking down our noses in disapproval because this or that church does something differently than we do, our attitudes often communicate the message that "we are more righteous than you." We focus more on our differences than on what we have in common: the good news of Jesus Christ. This is crucial because non-believers usually do not identify us as different churches or denominations, but they see us as one body: Christians. Why should the world trust us when we don't trust and support one another? Why should anyone believe our message unless they see it lived out in our lives?

In Ephesians 4:1-3, Paul gives the church some explicit instructions: "Lead a life worthy of the calling to which you have been called, with all humility and gentleness, with patience, bearing with one another in love, making every effort to maintain the unity of the Spirit in the bond of peace." The message here is that Christians—and the Church—are to be unified in Christ despite our differences. Even when we don't agree, we are to show love and respect for one another.

Paul goes on to tell us why: "There is one body and one Spirit, just as you were called to the one hope of your calling, one Lord, one faith, one baptism, one God and Father of all, who is above all and through all and in all" (Ephesians 4:4-6). Let's look at these a little closer:

One Body – the Church
One Spirit – the Holy Spirit, who dwells in all believers
One Hope – Eternal life
One Lord – Jesus Christ
One Faith – Salvation through the redemptive power of Jesus
One Baptism – Our baptism signifies our entrance into the family of God
One God – of all believers

Perhaps we ought to spend more time focusing on these things, which unite us as the body of Christ, and less time worrying about the things we do not agree on, striving for unity that accepts, even celebrates, our diversity.

On the last night of his life, Jesus himself prayed that we would do so: "My prayer is not for them alone. I pray also for those who will believe in me through their message, that all of them may be one, Father, just as you are in me and I am in you. May they also be in us so that the world may believe that you have sent me. I have given them the glory that you gave me, that they may be one as we are one. I in them and you in me. May they be brought to complete unity to let the world know that you sent me and have loved them even as you have loved me" (John 17: 20-23 NIV).

When we practice this love that we preach, first with one another and then with the world, our message will not seem like empty words but will have a power that can change the world.

Reaching Relevance

In today's culture, people ask two questions when evaluating an organization's message and making a decision about whether they should become involved. The first is "Is it real for today?" and the second is "What does it mean to me?" They are looking for relevance to today's culture, as well as to their lives as individuals.

The first question acknowledges that there is a "disconnect" between many churches and the people they want to reach. It is largely the result of the rapid pace of change in our culture contrasted with the hesitancy to change that exists in many organized church groups. We must be open to new forums and formats for doing church. Our culture is more diverse than ever before, language has changed, and technology is changing the way we communicate. We must respond to these changes and make our faith accessible, interesting, and relevant to new generations of believers.

With the second question, people are asking, "So what?" What relevance does our message have to their lives? If we preach and teach the Bible but do not show people who are listening how to apply these Scriptural precepts to their daily lives, our words become only theoretical concepts. We have to make sure we relate the good news of Jesus Christ to the context in which they live. This means addressing the complex and sometimes controversial issues they are faced with in the world. It also means being willing to meet them where they are—emotionally, spiritually, and physically. That's not easy and, in fact, can be downright scary, but it is so critical! If we make our message relevant, we can have a dramatic impact on people's lives; without relevance, we won't influence them at all.

Connecting People

In 1998, Christian sociologist George Barna published research in his book *The Second Coming of the Church* that revealed the "majority of people who made a first-time decision for Christ were no longer connected to a Christian church within just eight weeks of having made such a decision" ([Nashville: Word Publishing, 1998] p. 2). That's a staggering statistic! It is evidence that for many people who come through our doors, our churches are not making a lasting impact.

People lose their connection with the church for a variety of reasons. We fail to assimilate new believers into the body of Christ. Imagine this scenario. A couple visits a church for the first time. As visitors, they are greeted and made to feel welcomed. A few weeks later they join the church. After a month, they have not met any additional members of the church. No one has called to invite them to join a Sunday school class; and when they

came to the Wednesday night church dinner, no group invited them to join their table. How long do you think they will continue to attend this church? We need to reach out to people and encourage them to continue to grow in faith as part of our community. Does your church have the spiritual vitality that comes with ongoing discipleship and spiritual growth?

Now imagine a different scenario. In this one, someone walks into your church with green hair, multiple visible body piercings, and tattoos. How is this person greeted? As warmly as the conservatively dressed visitor who looks like everyone else? What would happen if a homeless man, who was dressed in rags and did not smell very good, attended your church? Would people sit by him, or would they give him a wide berth? While we tend to judge on outward appearances, God sees what is in the heart. What if a woman visited your church who "looked" normal but just didn't behave as you might expect? Would you be annoyed, glaring at her to send her a message? You know, the fact is that lost people act lost. Our task is not to judge but to show them the love of Jesus so that they will desire a connection with him and with his church. If we reject them, do you believe that will happen?

Churches also need to connect members into ministry. People are searching for meaning and purpose in life. They are getting involved in places where they feel they can fill a need, make a difference, and put their unique abilities to use. Our churches, however, fail to recognize this, too often thinking that the ministry of the church is to be done by the pastor and the church staff. This not only burns out our pastors and staff, but it also makes our members feel disconnected and unvalued. People who are connected and actively involved in an organization's work are also more committed to the organization.

Achieving Renewal

Thankfully, there are a significant number of people, both clergy and laity, who are committed to bringing renewal to our churches. There is no simple, quick fix approach to revitalization. What history tells us, though, is that renewal is achievable. As churches, we must be *the* church for people, modeling Christianity for the world (walking in a manner worthy of our calling), by striving for unity within our diversity. We must go out and make disciples, using a message that is authentic and relevant in today's world. We must be the body of Christ—open, connected, and interdependent. What can you, as an individual, do? First, understand your denomination's central doctrines. Accept that you will most likely never find any organized church where you will agree 100 percent with every detail of its doctrine. The question is whether or not there is enough agreement so that you can support your denomination publicly. As a leader, this is crucial! You have the ability to influence each person you are in contact with; so make sure you are a positive influence, and not a person who causes divisions (see Titus 3:9-11).

Second, encourage renewal and revitalization within your own congregation. You can do this in a variety of ways. Reach out to people you don't know; make newcomers feel welcome. Sometimes we feel so comfortable with our "group" that we fail to recognize it as a "clique" that makes others feel like outsiders. Invite others to get involved in ministry and discipleship with you. Spiritual vitality happens when we are connected to one another and to our church. As leaders, you have a responsibility to encourage others to use their spiritual gifts and to grow in their faith. Another thing you can do is to be open to change and new ways of doing things. Third, when you meet leaders from other churches or denominations, be open and generous in sharing both your ministry successes and mistakes. We can learn from one another. All Christian churches are part of the body of Christ; and if we can encourage and support each other's work, God's kingdom as a whole benefits.

Finally, preserve the "unity of the Spirit" as instructed in Ephesians 4:3-6: "Make every effort to keep the unity of the Spirit through the bond of peace. There is one body and one Spirit—just as you were called to one hope when you were called—one Lord, one faith, one baptism; one God and Father of all, who is over all and through all and in all." Do not allow yourself to get caught up in gossip or negative discussions about other churches or denominations. When you have conversations with a member of another denomination, focus more on those essential tenets of faith that we all have in common as believers in Christ, and spend less time worrying about the non-essentials about which we disagree.

Now let's turn to Scripture and review some passages that may have a message for us about what God expects from us as his church.

Biblical Foundation

As you review each Scripture passage, underline or circle key words or phrases. Note your insights in the space provided. What do these mean to your life, and to the life of your church? After you have finished reflecting on these passages and recording your insights, answer the questions that follow. We have included a passage from the book of Revelation. Although this passage was pulled from a letter written to a specific church, it has meaning for us today, too.

To the angel of the church in Sardis write: …I know your works; you have a name of being alive, but you are dead. Wake up and strengthen what remains and is on the point of death, for I have not found your works perfect in the sight of my God. Remember, then, what you have received and heard; obey it, and repent. (Revelation 3:1a, 2-3a)

"Here's another way to put it: You're here to be light, bringing out the God-colors in the world. God is not a secret to be kept. We're going public with this, as public as a city on a hill. If I make you light-bearers, you don't think I'm going to hide you under a bucket, do you? I'm putting you on a light stand. Now that I've put you there on a hilltop, on a light stand—shine! Keep open house; be generous with your lives. By opening up to others, you'll prompt people to open up with God, this generous Father in heaven." (Matthew 5:14-16 Msg.)

*They were continually devoting themselves to the apostles'
teaching and to fellowship, to the breaking of bread and to
prayer. …And all those who had believed were together and
had all things in common; and they began selling their
property and possessions and were sharing them with all, as
anyone might have need. Day by day continuing with one
mind in the temple, and breaking bread from house to house,
they were taking their meals together with gladness and
sincerity of heart, praising God and having favor with all
the people. And the Lord was adding to their number day by
day those who were being saved. (Acts 2:42, 43-47 NASB)*

*"My prayer is not for them alone. I pray also for those who
will believe in me through their message, that all of them
may be one, Father, just as you are in me and I am in you.
May they also be in us so that the world may believe that
you have sent me. I have given them the glory that you gave
me, that they may be one as we are one. I in them and you
in me. May they be brought to complete unity to let the
world know that you sent me and have loved them even as
you have loved me." (John 17: 20-23 NIV)*

*Make every effort to keep the unity of the Spirit through the
bond of peace. There is one body and one Spirit—just as you
were called to one hope when you were called—one Lord, one
faith, one baptism; one God and Father of all, who is over
all and through all and in all. (Ephesians 4:3-6 NIV)*

*Avoid foolish controversies and genealogies and arguments
and quarrels about the law, for these are unprofitable and
useless. Warn a divisive person once, and then warn [him or
her] a second time. After that, have nothing to do with [him
or her]. You may be sure that such a [person] is warped
and sinful. (Titus 3:9-11a NIV)*

Reflection Questions

1. The passage from Matthew 5:14-16 in the
   Message Bible says this: "Keep open house; be
   generous with your lives. By opening up to
   others, you'll prompt people to open up with God,
   this generous Father in heaven." How might this
   apply to renewal in our churches?

2. As described in Acts 2:42-47, the early church
   had a spirit of unity and togetherness, sharing all
   that they had. The New American Standard Bible
   states that they "day by day continued with one
   mind…" Do you think this means they agreed on
   every detail? Does any group of diverse people
   ever agree on every detail? What does it mean
   then to "continue with one mind"?

3. Before he was arrested, Jesus prayed that his
   disciples and all the believers who came after
   them would "be one," just as Jesus was one with
   the Father. Why do you think Jesus prayed this?

4. The passage you read from Ephesians 4:3-6
   instructs us to "make every effort to maintain the
   unity of the Spirit." Why is unity important? This
   passage also refers to seven characteristics
   common to all believers. What are they, and what
   is the significance?

5. The passage from Titus 3:9-11 tells us to avoid
   foolish controversies, arguments, and quarrels,
   "for these are unprofitable and useless." What
   does that mean to you as a leader?

HEART

Taking It to Heart

1. Which denominations and various churches have you been a part of—both past and current?

2. What do you appreciate most about each of them?

3. What does your church do to be relevant in today's world?

4. How does your church handle change? How do you handle change?

5. Describe your experience as a new person in your congregation. How did you get connected? If you have always been part of your congregation, describe how you became involved in ministry.

6. How do you reach out to others who may be looking for a connection in your church?

Heart to Heart

1. As a group, develop a two- to three-sentence summary of the video presentation.

2. Discuss the Scripture passages from this week's reading. Which ones spoke to you in some way, and why?

3. What can we do as individuals and leaders to preserve the "unity of the Spirit"—within our congregations and with other denominations? What impact might a unified church have on those outside of the church—namely, the people we are trying to reach?

4. Discuss what you as individual leaders can do to help people get connected with your congregation.

HANDS

Action Plan

1. Spend a few minutes reporting to your accountability partner(s) on your action plan from last week. Did you approach your small group or family or friends about doing a missions project? What was their response?

2. For next week, learn more about the policies and doctrines of your church or denomination. Ask an expert, visit a website, or check out a book from the library. Talk with your accountability partner(s) about specific questions you'd like to research, as well as ways to gather information. Be ready to report to your partner(s) next week one new thing you learned.

SESSION 8

AS EACH PART DOES ITS WORK

Serving in the Community Environment of Teams

Materials Needed:
◆ nametags
◆ pens or pencils
◆ TV and DVD player

For opening activity:
Your choice:
◆ One bag of marshmallows and a handful of thick spaghetti noodles for each group, OR
◆ Stack of index cards for each group

Room Set-up:

◆ Arrange pre-assigned groups around tables so that members are facing one another.
◆ Place TV and DVD player so that all can see (participants may need to turn their chairs around to view video).

Timing:

This outline is designed to cover a ninety-minute session. If you prefer to fit this into a sixty-minute format, we suggest deleting the Opening Activity and reducing the Heart to Heart Small Group Discussion to thirty minutes and the Hands Action Plan to ten minutes. If you prefer a two-hour format, include a fifteen-minute break after the Video Presentation Discussion, and add fifteen minutes to the Heart to Heart Small Group Discussion.

Opening Prayer and Welcome

(5 minutes)

Welcome participants to *Leadership from the Heart*, Session 8. The purpose of this session is to understand that teamwork is Jesus' model for ministry. As leaders, we are called to foster a healthy environment of teamwork.

Opening Activity

(15 minutes)

*Do not share the purpose of this activity with participants until after the activity is completed. Doing so will undermine the process of self-discovery, which is important for adult learning.

The purpose of this activity is to help participants realize that when they work synergistically, as a team, they are more successful.

Give each group either the marshmallows and dry spaghetti, or the index cards (whichever you use, give all the groups the same materials). Their challenge: As a group, build the tallest tower. Allow four minutes for the groups to complete the assignment.

Bring the full group back together. Congratulate all the groups on their efforts. Point out any unusual results, including tallest and "not-so-tall." Offer them an opportunity to try it again, but this time tell them they are to first discuss their results and strategize how to improve. Encourage all participants to take part in the discussion. Allow three minutes for the "strategy session." Call time, and tell them to begin construction. Give them another four minutes to complete the project.

Use the following questions to generate a short discussion (allow four minutes for this):

1. It looks like you were more successful the second time (*trust us, they will be*)! What happened?
2. What insights did you gain from this exercise?
3. How can you apply it to your leadership?

Video Presentation

Carol Cartmill (Approx. 9 minutes)

Play the video segment for Session 8.

Full Group Video Discussion

(5 minutes)

Facilitate a full group discussion based on the video presentation using the questions that follow. Don't be nervous if no one responds immediately. If there is a pause and you do not fill in the silence, someone eventually will speak up! After someone responds, ask for other comments. After one or two comments, go on to the next question, and so forth. Try to keep this initial discussion brief and to the point. Inform the participants that more in-depth discussion will follow in their small groups.

1. Jesus modeled team ministry for us. If he was willing to entrust his mission to a group of people who had proven to be less than reliable, we should be able to entrust the work of our ministry to a group of dedicated people. So, why do we struggle with that so much?
2. The speaker talked briefly about having a team of an appropriate size. What kinds of experiences have you had with teams that were either too large or too small?
3. Team ministry is more productive than individual ministry, but it is also more sustainable. Why is that?
4. What other insights or thoughts do you have regarding the video?

Bring the group back to this key point:
Team ministry is the biblical model for ministry. It has challenges and requires a lot of time and attention; but with a healthy team environment, the results are certainly worth the effort.

Heart to Heart Small Group Discussions

(40 minutes)

Each small group guide should start the discussion by reminding group members that the discussion questions are not designed to have "right" or "wrong" answers. They are meant to encourage group members to share their own insights and experiences, as well as what they've learned, so that members of the group can learn from one another. Everyone has something to offer! The guide should encourage each person to participate, and should keep any one individual from dominating the discussion. Refer to the Tips for Small Group Guides in this *Leader's Guide* (page 8) for pointers on group facilitation.

Begin by asking the group to summarize the video presentation. Groups should try to get that message into a few short sentences.

Ask group members which passage(s) from this week's Scripture spoke to them and why.

Continue the discussion using the Heart to Heart questions on page 101.

Hands Action Plan

(15 minutes)

Small group guides should direct group members to get with their accountability partner(s) and proceed with the Hands portion of the session on pages 102.

First, they each take one minute reporting their progress on last week's action plan. What did and did not happen as they had hoped?

Next, they take six to eight minutes developing their action plans for this week.

Finally, each one shares his or her action plan for the upcoming week.

Closing Circle Prayer

(5 minutes)

Small group guides should bring the accountability partners of the small groups back together for joys and concerns and a closing prayer. Ask the participants to keep their comments brief, encouraging them to share detailed prayer requests outside of class time—either in person, on the phone, or via e-mail.

We encourage you to use a circle prayer format to close the small group time. The

ability to lead a group prayer is essential in Christian leadership, but many people are not comfortable praying aloud. Circle prayers are useful in helping people become comfortable praying in a group. Remind the participants that their words do not have to be elaborate— just from the heart!

Have members stand, if they are able, holding hands around the table. Ask each person to speak one sentence in prayer, with the small group guide opening and closing the prayer.

AS EACH PART DOES ITS WORK

CHAPTER 8 Serving in the Community Environment of Teams

Speaking the truth in love, we will in all things grow up into him who is the Head, that is, Christ. From him the whole body, joined and held together by every supporting ligament, grows and builds itself up in love, as each part does its work.
(Ephesians 4:15-16 NIV)

 HEAD

Key Insights

◆ Churches that embrace team-based leadership are more healthy and effective in ministry.

◆ Servant-leaders recognize the importance of building up the body of Christ through team ministry and, consequently, work to develop the necessary heart and skills to build and sustain teams.

◆ God can accomplish much through individuals who seek his will, share responsibilities, encourage one another, serve in their areas of giftedness, and grow together.

Understanding the Concept

God created us for community. It only stands to reason, then, that God designed the church to meet the needs of the world through service done in community. Even God exists in community. Think about the Trinity. God the Father, Jesus Christ, and the Holy Spirit are three distinct persons yet one God, living together in perfect harmony and love. This is a helpful image for the kind of loving and intimate community we are to have in the church.

As the church, we are distinct individuals, yet one body bound together in a loving relationship.

Jesus modeled ministry in community. He selected twelve men we know as the disciples to share in his work, investing three years in their development. Eleven of these eventually became the nucleus for the early church, calling still others into ministry.

In previous chapters, we have considered some foundational truths about servant-leadership in community, including 1) Leaders need followers, and followers need leaders; and 2) At times we are leaders, while at other times we are followers. These dynamics take place most often within the context of teams. Learning how to effectively operate within the context of a team, build a team, and care for team members is crucial to our development as leaders in the church. In this chapter we will lay a foundation for team ministry and briefly cover the fundamentals of effective teams.

The Ministry Team Approach

As Ephesians 4:15-16 tells us, we are the body of Christ. This statement implies God designed the members of his church to function interdependently. Individual members of the body are given different and unique spiritual gifts. Just as God calls individuals to steward the gifts he has given them and employ those gifts to benefit others in the body of Christ, so God calls the church to steward the gifts of its members.

The church is most healthy and effective when all of the gifts given to its individual members are utilized and are operating in harmony with one another. As servant-leaders, we honor God when we take an active role in bringing forth the gifts of every member of the body, releasing individuals for meaningful, joyful, and effective ministry in community. We bring balance to our churches and ministries when we organize ourselves in ways that allow a variety of gifts to work together to fulfill the mission and ministry work of the church. After all, the way to determine the best organizational structure for a particular group is to look to the vision, purpose, mission, and values of the organization it represents. For groups within the church, who are working together to achieve a common purpose or goal, three types of structure are commonly chosen: committees, ad hoc groups (also referred to as task forces), and teams.

Committees are generally employed when the role they serve is one of oversight or governance, such as a Church Council, Finance Committee, Staff-Parish Relations Committee, or Building Committee. Some denominations mandate that particular ministry groups such as these operate as committees, and that the church body elects their members. When you look at the purposes of the aforementioned committees and the ways in which they function, it makes sense to elect members to these roles from across the landscape of the church. Each of the committees provides oversight to an important aspect of church "business" in support of ministry. For example, the Finance Committee governs and stewards the financial resources of the church by administering generally accepted accounting standards to financial reporting, reconciling church budgets and accounts, and keeping spending in line with the vision and purpose of the church and financial commitments of its members.

Ad hoc groups, or task forces, generally organize around a specified short-term goal or project. Committees may commission members to form an ad hoc committee, inviting individuals with certain expertise to work together on a specific project. Such groups have a clearly defined purpose. Once the goal is met, the group dissolves.

Teams are the most common form of structure utilized by effective churches and ministries. According to the Leadership Training Network, a *team* is a group of people with complimentary and diverse skills, gifts, and strengths who are committed to furthering a common purpose, supporting one another, achieving the team's mission, and holding one another accountable (*Growing Dynamic Teams*, [Dallas: Leadership Training Network] p. 16).

Team members often are recruited by personal invitation from within the ministry area where they currently serve or participate. Individually and collectively, they are "hands-on" in their approach to ministry; they "do" the work of ministry. In the team environment, individual members are developed, supported, cared for, and challenged. Because relationship building is integral to the health of the team, effective teams build in systems to provide for the growth of team members and the multiplication of their ministry. Team members serve both the church and one another in community.

> "People love to be encouraged. Great leaders know how to encourage others. They constantly praise others and build them up. They love to help others succeed and be their best.
> They exercise restraint in criticism but pursue praise and encouragement with a passion. Part of this quality and mission of encouraging others is used to mentor and develop other strong leaders around you. Successful leaders mentor others and help others hear God's call into ministry.Æ
>
> —Adam Hamilton, *Leading Beyond the Walls*

Ministry teams are usually comprised of no more than eight to twelve people. Having too many team members compromises the team leader's ability to provide adequate direction and care. As James White observes in his book *Rethinking the Church*, a ministry team is "nothing more than a small group of people with a complimentary assortment of gifts and abilities who are committed to a particular ministry that supports the purposes and mission of the church" ([Grand Rapids, MI: Baker Books, 1997] p. 102).

The Barna Research Group has studied the impact of ministry teams on churches both large and small. According to the results, "a large church that does not use teams will suffer. Specifically, its leaders will be burned out, the church's capacity to minister effectively will be limited, its senior pastor will become either a cult hero or blockage to the ministry process, and the ministry will become less participative" (George Barna, *The Power of Team Leadership: Finding Strength in Shared Responsibility* [Colorado Springs, CO: WaterBrook Press, 2001] p. 28). Small churches that are not team-led are destined to remain just that—small.

It is important to note that although the focus of this chapter is on ministry teams, many of the principles and values presented are transferable to other types of work groups, such as committees and task forces. Jesus challenges us to love God and love our neighbor regardless of the ministry setting in which we serve.

Attributes of a Healthy Team

George Cladis, senior pastor of a growing church in Darien, Connecticut, and author of *Leading the Team-Based Church*, describes seven attributes of healthy church ministry teams. Before you can begin the process of building a ministry team, it is important to understand what these attributes are, why they are important, and how you might go about developing them. Master these and you will be an effective team leader.

It is important to note, however, that team members share responsibility in ensuring the health of the team. You can provide developmental direction to the team and model the attributes of an effective team leader, but all team members must take ownership in the team's overall health and success. If you are shouldering all of the responsibility as the team leader, then you do not really have a team.

1. Covenant

Perhaps you think of examples from Scripture when you consider the word *covenant*. God made a covenant with Abraham in the Old Testament, promising Abraham that his descendants would be more numerous than the stars, and that through him nations would be blessed. We have the New Testament example of covenant in Jesus, when at the Last Supper he tells the disciples to "take and drink" the wine as a symbol of the new covenant in which we are offered redemption through his blood. These examples of covenant capture the love God has for us and help to define our relationship with God.

As covenant communities, teams express God's love as members grow in relationship with God and one another. They grow in God's love by worshipping, praying, and studying scripture together. They grow in relationship with one another as they practice Christian fellowship and provide support to fellow team members.

A team covenant expresses the shared purpose, values, and expectations or behaviors of its members. Used wisely, a team covenant creates a foundation of mutual trust, love of God and neighbor, encouragement, mission focus, and accountability. Have team members create the covenant together and revisit it whenever new people join the team, whenever there is conflict, and whenever it is time to evaluate the team's effectiveness (most teams do this annually). (An example of a team covenant is included on the resource DVD.)

2. Vision

Two things that help a church to experience success are the clarity of its purpose and the visionary leadership of its pastor and other key leaders. A central purpose statement should form and inform everything that takes place within the church, with every member of the church taking the purpose statement to heart.

Likewise, ministry teams should create both vision and mission statements in alignment with the purpose and the vision of the church. The vision of the team serves as its ongoing inspiration and "roadmap," providing the overall direction for ministry. The vision statement should answer the question "What do we want to be when we grow up as a ministry?" It looks one, two, even five years down the road and creates the picture of where the ministry is heading. Team members take ownership in doing "whatever it takes" for the vision to be realized.

Consider Nehemiah. He cast an inspiring vision before his team. He kept the vision for rebuilding the walls of Jerusalem in front of his team, reminding them of their purpose in times of difficulty. He put people to work on the part of the wall nearest their homes, making the vision "real" to them and ensuring they would be invested in the work they were doing.

The team mission statement reflects the operational side of the team—who we are as a team, what we do, why we do it, and whom we serve. The mission statement helps to keep the energies and efforts of the team on track, moving in the direction of accomplishing its goals and objectives and realizing its vision. We will explore the mission statement in greater detail later in the chapter.

3. Culture

Believers are described in 1 Peter 1 as "aliens" or "strangers" in this world. In Romans 12:2, we are admonished to "not be conformed to this world" but to "be transformed." Much of the ministry work we do runs counter to the culture we know in society. This is why culture is such an important attribute of ministry teams. An effective team creates a culture of God's love and presence—both in the church and in the community.

Culture can be defined as our "way of life" and includes such things as our values, behaviors, and social norms. Every team has its own culture—a set of norms that define its beliefs and values, and that are reflected in its actions. Likely, the culture will take shape as the team progresses through various stages of development. These stages are sometimes referred to as forming, storming, norming, and performing. Expect some turbulence as the team grows and settles on its identity. Raising a team is similar in many ways to raising a child.

While society might place a high value on independence, effective teams operate in an environment of interdependence. Teams think of "we first" as opposed to "me first." The team culture should be one of mutual love, respect, and grace.

As team leaders, we can affect the team's culture in a variety of ways. First, we can model Christian love and values in our own lives. The team can be intentional about creating an environment of Christian fellowship—breaking bread together, worshipping together, and praying for one another. Members can hold one another accountable to maintaining an outward focus and self-less attitude. Many of these values should be included in the team covenant and will affect team culture when they are lived out.

4. Collaboration

Teams are collaborative by nature. There are no superstars; all team members share in the blessings of ministry. Collaboration is essentially bringing spiritual gifts together to be used in ministry. It takes the very best of who God created each individual to be and puts to work the strengths of every member.

Individual team members are not in competition with one another. They may offer diversity in gifts and ideas, but they work together to bring about the best possible whole from the various parts offered. *All* gifts, abilities, ideas, talents, and contributions are celebrated in the team environment.

An orchestra makes beautiful music when all of the individual instruments play their parts in harmony. Think about an accomplishment that you played an instrumental part in, but that also required the contributions of others. It often works like that in ministry. One person can dream up and execute an idea well, but the dream really takes flight when multiple persons pour themselves into it. As a servant-leader, you are called to be a role model in this attribute as you encourage, recognize, and celebrate the contributions of individual team members, giving team members credit where and when it is due.

5. Trust

Team members must be able to trust one another. Community can be built and sustained only in an atmosphere of trust. Likewise, community is torn apart in the presence of lies and deceit. Ministry is often risky business. People who cannot trust in those with whom they serve are not likely to take reasonable risks, which are often necessary to move a ministry forward. Once trust is broken, it is very difficult to reestablish. It takes time for the community to be healed.

As a team leader, you must maintain your own integrity and be absolutely worthy of the trust others place in you. It has been said people will follow a leader anywhere when they trust that the leader has their best interests at heart.

6. Empowerment

The very word "empowerment" conjures up images of power being given away to others. It is the responsibility of team members to give away power, including the rights to personally control the tasks of ministry. The irony in this is that when all the team members are truly empowered, very little thought and energy is spent on worrying about who is in control.

Empowering others is difficult for some leaders, but it is essential. Moses is a good example. In Exodus 18, Jethro, Moses' father-in-law, finds Moses presiding over all decisions, with long lines of people waiting to see him. his advice to Moses is this: "What you are doing is not good. You will surely wear yourself out, both you and these people with you. The task is too heavy for you; you cannot do it alone" (Ex. 18:17b-18). He then tells Moses to appoint other people, train them to handle disputes, and appoint them to preside over the decisions. The result, he says, will be that "all these people will go to their home in peace" and Moses will be free to do other things (v. 23).

The task of the team leader is to help others become all God intended for them to be. Effective teams create an environment of empowerment where the gifts and passions of its members can be fully realized. Wayne Cordeiro, pastor of New Hope Church in Hawaii, refers to leaders who empower others as "dream releasers." In his book *Doing Church as a Team*, he writes, "God calls every leader to be a dream releaser. There is nothing more spectacular than seeing people's dreams released and being used for the glory of God! There is no greater joy!" ([Honolulu: New Hope Resources, 1998] p. 111)

Becoming a servant-leader who is a dream-releaser takes intentional effort. The leader must be aware of the dreams of individual team members; the gifts and talents possessed by each team member; and the planning, support, and resources team members will need in order for their dreams to be realized.

7. Learning

Dynamic churches value creativity and innovation. They encourage members of ministry teams to hunger after knowledge, both spiritual and practical; to pursue opportunities to put that knowledge to good use; and to seek places where they can continually experience growth. Teams that learn together grow together and stay together.

Spiritual learning can take place in some form at every team gathering when members of the team share the responsibility of leading devotions. Teams may decide to engage in book studies, reading one or more chapters of an agreed upon book between meetings and devoting part of the agenda to discussing individual insights from what has been read. Some might choose to attend training workshops or conferences together, followed by a special gathering to debrief, share knowledge, and plan for ways to put new ideas into practice. Teams also might invite guest speakers—pastors or other leaders—to teach at their meetings or retreats.

Keys to Operating an Effective Team

Now that we have considered the attributes of healthy teams, it is time to shift our focus to the more operational side of teamwork. Sustaining healthy, effective teams takes intentional effort. Keys to operating an effective team include the following:

- Team Mission Statement and Team Member Role Descriptions
- Effective Communication and Decision Making
- Balanced Participation and Shared Leadership
- Effective Meetings
- Tools to Measure Progress

Although we will consider each of these key processes involved in building and operating an effective ministry team, we acknowledge that team building is much more of an organic process than one of mere mechanics.

Team Mission Statement and Team Member Role Descriptions

Just as an effective church provides written guidelines for servant-leaders (including the purpose statement, vision, mission, and values of the church, as well as expectations for church members and servant-leaders), an effective ministry team develops a defined ministry mission statement along with position descriptions for the various roles within the team. These documents serve as both invitation and evaluation tools.

Having a clear mission statement helps a team understand what it is called to do and why. The team uses this statement to keep its focus, establish boundaries for what is and is not included in its work, understand where its work fits within the overall purpose and vision of the church, and define and evaluate success.

Of course, a team mission statement always should be in alignment with the purpose, vision, and values of the church. A properly developed team mission statement also answers four key questions:

- *What do we call ourselves — what is the name of our team or ministry?*
- *Who is our customer — who is being served by our ministry?*
- *What do we do — how would we describe our ministry work?*
- *Why do we do it — what is our motivation?*

The answers to these questions should be concise and "to the point" so that the mission statement is easily understood by people both inside and outside the ministry. A well-written mission statement gives a team a firm foundation. (A mission statement template is included on the resource DVD.)

In addition to defining the work of the ministry team, it is important to define the roles of individual team members. Before you can invite someone into a ministry role, you first must set appropriate guidelines and expectations for that role. The purpose of a ministry position description is similar to that of a mission statement. It, too, provides focus and sets boundaries. A position description should include the title of the position; the ministry area; the name and title of the person to whom the position is responsible; a brief description of the tasks and responsibilities of the position; a list of the desired qualifications, including gifts, talents, style, passion, experience, and training; regular commitments, such as team meetings; and a realistic estimate of the time commitment involved. (A sample team member role description can be found on the resource DVD.) Team members should be aware of the roles and responsibilities of every member of the team.

Effective Communication and Decision Making

A great deal of misunderstanding and heartache can be avoided by developing effective communication skills. A servant-leader must be adept at personal communication. This involves both speaking and listening skills. You must be clear — and, preferably, concise — when communicating to others. You also must practice "active listening" when others are speaking with you — as opposed to passive listening, in which you are engaged in multitasking or are tuned out. When communicating with others, be sure to check for understanding by asking questions that ensure the other person has received the message as you intended it. (If this is an area in which you struggle, seriously consider taking a course or attending a workshop to help you develop in this area.)

Have a plan for communication outside meetings. Ask yourself, *How will progress on various ministry tasks be communicated to team members between meetings?*

Many teams work well utilizing e-mail updates. Think about how church news and information might be disseminated to the group. Capture important meeting details and assignments in writing, distribute these to everyone, and invite feedback. Develop a system to follow up with individuals who miss important meetings or events. Be sure to distribute to all team members a contact sheet that includes names, phone numbers, e-mail addresses, and ministry positions.

Take time to discuss and decide how your team will make decisions. This may depend upon the type of decision being made. Some decisions might be critical enough to warrant a unanimous decision by all team members. In most cases, however, consensus is enough. There may be times when the group will want to defer a decision to just one person. The point here is to have the discussion before the decision must be made. Clarity on this one issue can help the team avoid potential conflict. Once a team becomes established, decision-making will become second-nature.

Balanced Participation and Shared Leadership

Individual team members possess different gifts and styles. Not every team member will participate in exactly the same manner. Strive for balanced participation, where every team member is actively contributing to discussions and workload in harmony with his or her gifting and style. Some members may feel comfortable sharing in discussions only when they have special expertise or insight relating to the topic. Find ways to draw out quiet team members without putting them on the spot, and to quiet the most vocal members without causing them embarrassment. This can be partially achieved when the team creates its covenant and establishes its ground rules and values. Issues such as showing respect for all opinions and valuing all voices can be raised at that time.

An element that sets ministry teams apart from individual ministry is shared leadership. Help team members take responsibility and leadership for areas of team building within their areas of gifting. If someone excels at communication, he or she might be responsible for team communication. Someone with the gifts of encouragement and helps might take responsibility for fellowship and social activities. Individuals with a heart for teaching and education might take responsibility for the group's shared learning experiences, and so on.

This same philosophy also applies to the ministry tasks of the team as defined by its mission statement. Likely, every team has elements of administration, prayer, communication, service, and a whole host of tasks to accomplish. Each team member should take the lead in an area of God-given strength.

Effective Meetings

Ineffective meetings can derail ministry and create stress. There is a science to facilitating effective meetings. Fortunately, these skills can be learned. Here are a few simple meeting guidelines:

◆ Use an *agenda*. The agenda should include the date, time, and location of the meeting; the purpose for the meeting; discussion topics, time estimates for each topic, and the name of the person leading each topic's discussion. Distribute the agenda in advance of the meeting, preferably a week ahead as a reminder. Be careful to create a realistic agenda—not too many topics, with enough time for each.

◆ Start the meeting with *prayer*. Try to include a brief devotion as well.

◆ Plan a *warm up* activity. People need to mentally transition from the last activity of the day. This may be a simple "check in" where each person tells the best thing to happen to them, or where they have seen God working in the last week.

◆ Facilitate effective *discussion*, trying to involve all the members of the team. Be sure to practice active listening and to clarify issues when necessary.

◆ Manage the *time*. Stick to the agenda. If the group starts to get off topic, utilize a "parking lot" method where you can "park" ideas not relating to the agenda for discussion at a different time.

◆ Reach *decisions*. Follow the agreements outlined in the team covenant so that you may walk away from the meeting having made decisions. Be specific about decisions and assignments by including time frames and target goals. People feel good about walking away from meetings when this happens.

◆ Keep *records*. If decisions and assignments were made, be sure to capture those in writing. Keeping good records also helps new team leaders and members in the future.

◆ Provide an element of *fellowship*. This may be food, a game, a learning opportunity, or a time of sharing personal joys and concerns. This is how teams cultivate an environment of care for one another and display the love of God.

◆ *Evaluate* every meeting. A simple way to do this is to have everyone in the room verbally rate the meeting on a scale of 1 to 10, with 10 being the best. Go around the room a second time, giving each person the opportunity to share briefly what would have made the meeting a "10" for him or her.

Tools to Measure Progress

As team leader, take time occasionally—quarterly, at a minimum—to guide the team in evaluating the team's progress in light of previously agreed upon goals and objectives. In addition, plan to conduct one-on-one evaluations with every team member on an annual basis. The purpose of these individual evaluations is to affirm individual contributions, measure growth and progress, and reaffirm commitment to the ministry of the team. Recognize that there will be times when a team member may need to take a sabbatical from the team's ministry or consider a new or different challenge. (Sample evaluation tools can be found on the resource DVD.)

Because we were created for community, ministry teams are the optimal environment for fostering Christian service. Jesus modeled it, and the church would do well to heed his example. As servant-leaders, we can maximize the impact of ministry by helping to build healthy teams and invest in team members.

Biblical Foundation

As you review each Scripture passage, underline or circle key words or phrases. Think about the implications of each passage for your life, noting your insights in the space provided. Answer the questions that follow.

Speaking the truth in love, we will in all things grow up into him who is the Head, that is, Christ. From him the whole body, joined and held together by every supporting ligament, grows and builds itself up in love, as each part does its work. (Ephesians 4:15-16 NIV)

So I came to Jerusalem and was there for three days. Then I got up during the night, I and a few men with me; I told no one what my God had put into my heart to do for Jerusalem. The only animal I took was the animal I rode. I went out by night by the Valley Gate past the Dragon's Spring and to the Dung Gate, and I inspected the walls of Jerusalem that had been broken down and its gates that had been destroyed by fire. Then I went on to the Fountain Gate and to the King's Pool; but there was no place for the animal I was riding to continue. So I went up by way of the valley by night and inspected the wall. Then I turned back and entered by the Valley Gate, and so returned. The officials did not know where I had gone or what I was doing; I had not yet told the Jews, the priests, the nobles, the officials, and the rest that were to do the work. Then I said to them, "You see the trouble we are in, how Jerusalem lies in ruins with its gates burned. Come, let us rebuild the wall of Jerusalem, so that we may no longer suffer disgrace." I told them that the hand of God had been gracious upon me, and also the words that the king had spoken to me. Then they said, "Let us start building!" So they committed themselves to the common good. *(Nehemiah 2:11-18)*

So we rebuilt the wall, and all the wall was joined together to half its height; for the people had a mind to work. But when Sanballat and Tobiah and the Arabs and the Ammonites and the Ashdodites heard that the repairing of the walls of Jerusalem was going forward and the gaps were beginning to be closed, they were very angry, and all plotted together to come and fight against Jerusalem and to cause confusion in it. So we prayed to our God, and set a guard as a protection against them day and night. But Judah said, "The strength of the burden bearers is failing, and there is too much rubbish so that we are unable to work on the wall. And our enemies said, "They will not know or see anything before we come upon them and kill them and stop the work." When the Jews who lived near them came, they said to us ten times, "From all the places where they live they will come up against us." So in the lowest parts of the space behind the wall, in open places, I stationed the people according to their families, with their swords, their spears, and their bows. After I looked these things over, I stood up and said to the nobles and the officials and the rest of the people, "Do not be afraid of them. Remember the Lord, who is great and awesome, and fight for your kin, your sons, your daughters, your wives, and your homes." When our enemies heard that their plot was known to us, and that God had frustrated it, we all returned to the wall, each to his work. From that day on, half of my servants worked on construction, and half held spears, shields, bows, and body-armor; and the leaders posted themselves behind the whole house of Judah, who were building the wall. The burden bearers carried their loads in such a way that each labored on the work with one hand and with the other held a weapon. And each of the builders had his sword strapped at his side while he built. *(Nehemiah 4:6-18a)*

The next day Moses sat as judge for the people, while the people stood around him from morning until evening. When Moses' father-in-law saw all that he was doing for the people, he said, "What is this you are doing for the people? Why do you sit alone, while all the people stand around you from morning until evening?" Moses said to his father-in-law, "Because the people come to me to inquire of God. When they have a dispute, they come to me, and I decide between one person and another, and I make known to them the statutes and instructions of God." Moses father-in-law said to him, "What you are doing is not good. You will surely wear yourself out, both you and these people with you. The task is too heavy for you; you cannot do it alone. Now listen to me and I will give you counsel, and God be with you! You should represent the people before God and bring their cases before him; teach them the statutes and instructions, and make known to them the way they are to go and the things they are to do. You should also look for able men among all the people, men who fear God, are trustworthy, and who hate dishonest gain; set such men over them as officers over thousands, hundreds, fifties and tens. Let them sit as judges for the people at all times, let them bring every important case to you, but decide every minor case themselves. So it will be easier for you, and they will bear the burden with you. If you do this and God so commands you, then you will be able to endure, and all these people will go to their home in peace." So Moses listened to his father-in-law and did all that he had said. Moses chose able men from all Israel and appointed them as heads over the people, as officers over thousands, hundreds, fifties and tens. And they judged the people at all times; hard cases they brought to Moses, but any minor case they decided themselves. *(Exodus 18:13-26)*

[Jesus] went up the mountain and called to him those whom he wanted, and they came to him. And he appointed twelve, who he also named apostles, to be with him and to be sent out to proclaim the message and to have authority to cast out demons. *(Mark 3:13-15)*

Two are better than one, because they have a good return for their work: If one falls down, his friend can help him up. But pity the man who falls down and has no one to help him up! Also, if two lie down together, they will keep warm. But how can one keep warm alone? Though one may be overpowered, two can defend themselves. A cord of three strands is not quickly broken. (Ecclesiastes 4:9-12 NIV)

Without counsel plans go wrong, but with many advisers they succeed. (Proverbs 15:22)

How very good and pleasant it is when kindred live together in unity! (Psalm 133:1)

Reflection Questions

1. Describe the advantages of "each part [doing] its work" as gleaned from Ephesians 4:15-16.

2. The entire Book of Nehemiah is an excellent study in spiritual leadership. What were some of the basic keys and principles of leadership from your readings of Chapters 2 and 4 that led to the successful rebuilding of the wall in Jerusalem?

3. What was happening in Exodus 18 when Moses was trying to do all the work alone? What were the results when he implemented Jethro's model for ministry? What does this teach us about leadership, organizational structure, and ministry effectiveness?

4. What was Jesus' model for doing ministry (Mark 3:13-15)?

5. What advice does the writer of Ecclesiastes give with regard to "going it alone"? What are the advantages of seeking companions?

6. "Two heads are better than one" is an old and familiar saying. How does it compare with the advice given in Proverbs 15:22?

7. How might our "living in unity" (working together in teams) make us and our church more attractive to those outside our walls?

 # HEART

Taking It to Heart

1. Has the concept of serving in community ever occurred to you? Why or why not?

2. People sometimes employ a "pros and cons" list to help them make a decision. In the space below, list the pros and cons of the ministry team approach. After you have completed the list, try

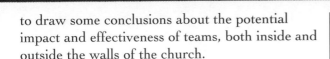

to draw some conclusions about the potential impact and effectiveness of teams, both inside and outside the walls of the church.

Pros	Cons

What did you conclude?

3. Have you ever participated on a team, either at church or elsewhere? If yes, describe the experience, including how you felt and what were the successes and challenges of the team and its leader. If not, what has prevented you from doing so?

4. Have you ever been frustrated when an individual could not minister to you in a timely manner? What might have prevented him or her from doing so? (Consider things such as work habits, environment, circumstances, and so forth.) Has there ever been a time when you caused someone else frustration by being unable to meet a ministry need in a timely manner? How might sharing ministry responsibilities with the members of a team circumvent this type of frustration? *Note: When answering these questions,*

assume that the expectations of the party seeking help are realistic. Think about Moses and Nehemiah.

Heart to Heart

1. As a group, develop a two- to three-sentence summary of the video presentation.

2. Discuss the Scripture passages from this week's reading. There are numerous examples of team ministry in the readings, including Jesus' choosing of twelve men to walk with him in ministry. Discuss the implications, both then and now, of his doing so.

3. Discuss the importance, benefits, and challenges of team ministry. Include examples from your personal experiences.

4. Talk about what might prevent leaders from building ministry teams. Are such leaders being shortsighted or realistic? Why?

5. Respond to the following questions:

How would you describe the worst team you have ever been a part of?

How would you describe the best team you have ever been a part of?

How would you describe the characteristics of an ideal team?

How would you describe the characteristics of an ideal team leader?

 **HANDS**

Action Plan

1. Share with your accountability partner(s) one new thing you learned during the week about the policies and doctrines of your church or denomination.

2. Make a list of all of the ministries you can think of in your church that utilize a team approach. Share this list with your accountability partner(s).

Team-based Ministries List:

3. During the week, select the one ministry you perceive to be the most effective and conduct a thorough investigation, drawing at least three conclusions about what makes this team so effective. Be prepared to share your conclusions about the effective team you chose with your accountability partner(s) next week. Take it a step further and challenge each other to name and implement at least one of the successful team-building steps in your own ministry. Make your goal specific and timely.

Example and Description of an Effective Team Ministry:

Reasons for Success:

Successful Team-building Step to Implement:

Related Goal:

SESSION 9

SO THAT THE BODY OF CHRIST MAY BE BUILT UP

Preparing God's People to Serve

Materials Needed:
◆ nametags
◆ pens or pencils
◆ TV and DVD player

For opening activity:
◆ photocopies of the "My Ministry: Thirty-second Commercial" worksheet for every participant (see DVD)

For next week's opening activity (see note at end of notes for this session):
◆ index cards (Each participant will need a stack of index cards—one card for every person in the small group except for himself or herself. For example, a small group of eight people would need fifty-six cards, and a small group of four people would need twelve cards.)

Room Set-up:
◆ Arrange pre-assigned groups around tables so that members are facing one another.
◆ Place TV and DVD player so that all can see (participants may need to turn their chairs around to view video).

Timing:
This outline is designed to cover a ninety-minute session. If you prefer to fit this into a sixty-minute format, we suggest deleting the Opening Activity and reducing the Heart to Heart Small Group Discussion to thirty minutes and the Hands Action Plan to ten minutes. If you prefer a two-hour format, include a fifteen-minute break after the Video Presentation Discussion, and add fifteen minutes to the Heart to Heart Small Group Discussion.

Opening Prayer and Welcome
(5 minutes)
Welcome participants to *Leadership from the Heart*, Session 9. The purpose of this session is to discover that, as leaders, we have a responsibility not only to get people in the right positions, but also to equip them to serve and to sustain them with encouragement and caring.

Opening Activity
(10 minutes)
Do not share the purpose of this activity with participants until after the activity is completed. Doing so will undermine the process of self-discovery, which is important for adult learning.

The purpose of this activity is to give participants the hands-on experience of creating a clear, concise, and compelling statement about the ministry area in which they serve. This is a valuable invitation tool for recruiting potential volunteers. This same tool can be adapted for use whenever the leader of a ministry needs to communicate with others the vision and impact of his or her ministry. Leaders are sometimes asked to share the vision for their ministry at a moment's notice and must be prepared to do so. Unexpected opportunities to invite new people into ministry sometimes present themselves. It's important to be ready when they do!

Give each group enough copies of the "My Ministry: Thirty-second Commercial" worksheet so that every member has his or her own copy. Tell participants they will have three to four minutes to complete the worksheet, after which they will be asked to share their work. When the time is up, have each group

member take turns delivering his or her commercial at their table. The group will vote on one commercial from their table to share with the larger group. Remember: The commercials should be thirty seconds or less in duration. Have fun and be encouraging. Creating a thirty-second commercial gets easier with practice.

Bring the full group back together. Have the "winner" from each table share his or her thirty-second commercial. Encourage members of all small groups to participate in expressing appreciation for the commercials through applause.

Use the following questions to generate a short discussion (allow four minutes for this):

1. How did the different commercials reflect our individuality?
2. Why is it important to be ready articulate our ministry work in a clear, concise, and compelling way?
3. Once you create your thirty-second commercial, how and where might you put it to use?

Video Presentation

Gia Garey (Approx. 6 minutes)

Play the video segment for Session 9.

Full Group Video Discussion

(5 minutes)

Facilitate a full group discussion based on the video presentation using the questions that follow. Don't be nervous if no one responds immediately. If there is a pause and you do not fill in the silence, someone eventually will speak up! After someone responds, ask for other comments. After one or two comments, go on to the next question, and so forth. Try to keep this initial discussion brief and to the point. Inform the participants that more in-depth discussion will follow in their small groups.

1. The speaker discussed a four-step process for holistic volunteer management: Invite, Connect, Equip, and Sustain. Why do you think all four stages are important?
2. She went on to say that many churches stop after the "connect" step, leaving out equipping and sustaining. In most churches, it is at least done inconsistently. Why do you think this is so? What experiences have you had with these four steps?
3. What other insights did you glean from this video?

Bring the group back to this key point:

If we are to have healthy teams, we must manage our team members holistically, making them feel valued, empowered, and cared for, instead of just plugging them in and burning them out.

Heart to Heart Small Group Discussions

(40 minutes)

Each small group guide should start the discussion by reminding group members that the discussion questions are not designed to have "right" or "wrong" answers. They are meant to encourage group members to share their own insights and experiences, as well as what they've learned, so that members of the group can learn from one another. Everyone has something to offer! The guide should encourage each person to participate, and should keep any one individual from dominating the discussion. Refer to the Tips for Small Group Guides in this *Leader's Guide* (page 8) for pointers on group facilitation.

Begin by asking the group to summarize the video presentation. Groups should try to get that message into a few short sentences.

Ask group members which passage(s) from this week's Scripture spoke to them and why.

Continue the discussion using the Heart to Heart questions on page 115.

Hands Action Plan

(15 minutes)

Small group guides should direct group members to get with their accountability partner(s) and proceed with the Hands portion of the session on page 115.

First, they each take one minute reporting their progress on last week's action plan. What did and did not happen as they had hoped?

Next, they take six to eight minutes developing their action plans for this week.

Finally, each one shares his or her action plan for the upcoming week.

Closing Circle Prayer

(5 minutes)

Small group guides should bring the accountability partners of the small groups back together for joys and concerns and a closing prayer. Ask the participants to keep their comments brief, encouraging them to share detailed prayer requests outside of class time — either in person, on the phone, or via e-mail.

We encourage you to use a circle prayer format to close the small group time. The ability to lead a group in prayer is essential in Christian leadership, but many people are not comfortable praying aloud. Circle prayers are useful in helping people become comfortable praying in a group. Remind the participants that their words do not have to be elaborate — just from the heart!

Have members stand, if they are able, holding hands around the table. Ask each person to speak one sentence in prayer, with the small group guide opening and closing the prayer.

*Note: Before the session closes this week, we recommend that you discuss the opening activity for Session 10 with the whole group so that they can be prepared. Session 10 discusses caring for the people we lead. In the opening activity, participants will provide encouragement and affirmation to the members of their small group by sharing one attribute they appreciate about each person, or one thing they have learned from each person. We suggest that you give each participant one index card for each member of their group. Before the next session, they should write their message of encouragement or affirmation on the index card. At the completion of the opening activity, they will give the written messages to the proper recipients for them to keep.

CHAPTER 9

SO THAT THE BODY OF CHRIST MAY BE BUILT UP
Preparing God's People to Serve

It was [Christ] who gave some to be apostles, some to be prophets, some to be evangelists, and some to be pastors and teachers, to prepare God's people for works of service, so that the body of Christ may be built up until we all reach unity in the faith and in the knowledge of the Son of God and become mature, attaining to the whole measure of the fullness of Christ.
(Ephesians 4:11-13)

HEAD

Key Insights

◆ Churches that embrace holistic volunteer practices are more healthy and effective in ministry.

◆ Servant-leaders recognize the importance of inviting, connecting, equipping, and sustaining others into the ministry of service and, consequently, work to develop the necessary heart and skills to support the volunteer management efforts of the church.

◆ God can accomplish much more when *all* members of the body of Christ are fulfilling the purpose for which they were created—serving by using their God-given gifts and talents.

Understanding the Concept

There is great diversity within the body of Christ. When you think about the human body and its many parts—from tiny lashes that protect our eyes to little toes that help us keep our balance—you cannot help but be amazed at God's care and creativity. So it goes with the church: Many different and unique members are gathered into one body. There are blessings and challenges with this truth. We are blessed as Christian communities to have access to God's power through the individual spiritual gifting of our members. When our members discover, develop, and deploy their spiritual gifts in service, our churches and communities benefit. God truly can accomplish so much more when all our members' gifts are yielded in his service. The challenge lies in activating all those uniquely gifted and created members. Members are not always aware of the roles they were created to fulfill.

The focus of this chapter is to prepare you, as a servant-leader, to help the members of your church body become actively engaged in the ministry of service. We discussed in a previous chapter the important role spiritual gifts discovery plays in connecting potential volunteers with meaningful places of ministry, but spiritual gifts are just one piece of a larger puzzle. The task is not done when you identify individuals' gifts and connect them into a place of ministry that matches their gifts. Then they must be trained and resourced to be effective in their new volunteer roles, and cared for so that they don't burn out serving the needs of others. This calls for a holistic approach to the way we *manage* our volunteers.

Our use of the words *manage* and *management* is deliberate. Management is the art, act, or manner of directing. It involves skill and careful treatment. Managing volunteers takes thoughtful planning. When it is well done, an effective volunteer management system is seamless and invisible to the volunteer. By that, we mean the volunteer doesn't notice or think about the "system" but places his or her focus on the ministry and the people being served. A good system for volunteer management can be described in four simple steps: 1) invite, 2) connect, 3) equip, and 4) sustain.

Step 1: Invite

Jesus invited people to "follow him" at the start of his three-year ministry (see Mark 1:17). It is where we begin, as well. The first step in volunteer management is *invite,* and it is all the word implies. We assess opportunities for the service involvement of others, define the mission of the particular ministry, clarify individual roles within the ministry, identify people to invite, and actually extend the invitation. Let's look at each of the components separately.

Assess the Opportunities

It probably was not a "spur of the moment" decision when Jesus invited those who would become his disciples to follow him. We read in the first chapter of John, verses 35 and following, the story of the calling of Andrew. Andrew had been one of John the Baptist's disciples and spent time with Jesus before becoming a disciple. Although the scriptures do not convey Jesus' thought processes, it is probable that Jesus had in mind places of service for each disciple he invited to follow him. The conversation between Peter and Jesus in John 21 implies Jesus had foreknowledge of the future for each disciple. Jesus spoke, in particular, of the manner of death for both Peter and John. Jesus knew where their ministry would take his disciples.

Likewise, before we can invite people to join us in ministry, we must give thought to what service opportunities exist. For example, a leader in Children's Ministry might identify a need for twelve Sunday school teachers, one administrator, five drama team members, six nursery workers, and so forth. Define your needs as specifically as possible. Quantify the opportunities for service, and set target dates for filling open positions.

Define the Mission

We described in Chapter 8 the process of developing vision and mission statements for ministry teams. As you will recall, the vision of a team serves as its ongoing inspiration and "roadmap," providing the overall direction for ministry. The team mission statement reflects the operational side of the team: who we are as a team, what we do, why we do it, and whom we serve. By providing this definition, you are describing for the potential volunteer what he or she is being invited to support through his or her service, enabling the individual to feel good about supporting the work of the particular ministry area and the overall church. (See the resource DVD for a mission statement template.)

Describe the Role

An important invitation tool is a written ministry position description, which we discussed in the previous chapter. (A sample can be found on the resource DVD.) Again, the position description should include the title of the position; the ministry area; the name and title of the person to whom the position is responsible; a brief description of the tasks and responsibilities of the position; a list of the desired qualifications, including gifts, talents, style, passion, experience, and training; regular commitments, such as team meetings; and a realistic estimate of the time commitment.

A ministry position description helps the ministry leader develop a profile of what to look for in a potential volunteer candidate and provides the candidate with honest and objective data to be used in making a thoughtful and prayerful decision about whether or not to accept the position. (See the resource DVD for a sample ministry position role description.)

Invite People into Ministry

Once you have defined the mission of the ministry and the requirements of the volunteer service positions, you are ready to extend invitations to those you would like to join the team. You will want to consider giftedness, availability, and several other factors when identifying and inviting people. Here are a few suggestions for identifying people to invite:

Pray. Be specific and persistent with God in your requests for new people to add to your volunteer team or church committee, and then be open to the possibilities of the people God might choose. God might place someone in your path you would have overlooked.

Ask other leaders. Since it is impossible to know everyone in most churches, ask other leaders and team members to help you identify potential team members. Every person has a unique sphere of influence; he or she may rub shoulders with an entirely different group of people. Identifying new candidates should be the work of every person serving in ministry.

Look for individuals who are...

◆ **Committed**. These are people who are faithful in worship and program attendance and are enthusiastic about their involvement in the church.

◆ **Spiritually mature**. Are there visible signs of a growing, deepening relationship with God? If the fruit of the Spirit—love joy, peace patience, etc.—is evident in the life of someone, chances are he or she is maturing spiritually.

◆ **Secure.** People with healthy self-esteem are ideal candidates for service roles.

◆ **Spiritually gifted.** Is your team in need of administrative help? Seek someone with the spiritual gift of administration. Pray for the wisdom and discernment to know exactly which gifts are needed on your team to help it function most effectively, and then seek individuals with those gifts.

◆ **Supportive of the church's vision.** People who embrace the purpose, vision, mission, and values of the church will make great additions to the volunteer roles of your church. If someone seriously struggles with the direction the church is taking, he or she may cause dissension.

◆ **Active and eager listeners.** Look for people who listen more than they talk, and who are open to learning new skills and embracing new ideas.

◆ **Problem solvers.** It is easy to point out shortcomings and mistakes. Problem solvers challenge ideas in a positive way and offer solutions.

After identifying a potential team member, you are ready to extend an invitation. Here are some suggestions:

1. Take the time to personally invite the person and share the vision of the ministry you represent. Remember that people will not commit if the cause is not compelling.

2. Learn about each one you invite so you can authentically affirm the gifts you see in him or her. Share with the person why you believe his or her gifts would compliment the team.

3. Use the written position description to dialogue with the individual about the ministry opportunity. Carefully explain the responsibilities of the team role and outline the support he or she will receive from you and the church in that role.

4. Pray for the individual and ask him or her to pray about committing to serve on the team.

5. Let the person know how important it is to have a singular focus for one ministry area. Though each individual decides how much time he or she can devote to the church, it is unhealthy when people spread themselves too thin due to over-commitment.

6. Follow up within a mutually agreed upon timeframe. Thank the individual for considering a

role on your ministry team, whether or not he or she accepts the position.

7. If the person says yes, take time at the next team meeting to build community between the new member and the existing team members. When a new person joins a team, it is a good time for all to revisit and affirm the mission of the team and the team covenant.

Remember: Every believer is ripe with potential. Effective servant-leaders take the time to find places of service where people can thrive based upon their giftedness. Be prepared, however, to overcome the objections of reluctant volunteers. Many people have trouble envisioning themselves serving in the church. If it is an issue of lack of confidence, you will have to help the person see that he or she is a gifted member of the body of Christ. Affirm the individual's gifts and offer support.

Step 2: Connect

Perhaps you can relate to this experience. You made a trip to the grocery store where you bought loads of food. While there, you decided to buy some fresh strawberries. They were ripe and red, and you couldn't wait to use them in a new strawberry shortcake recipe. But somehow those beautiful strawberries ended up buried in the back of the refrigerator where they remained "lost" for several weeks. By the time you discovered them, they were covered in mold—no longer fit for use. What a waste of time and money!

When people respond to our invitation to serve and we fail to connect them with a meaningful ministry opportunity, it's a much, much bigger waste than rotting food—and one with serious implications. A holistic volunteer management system includes a plan to connect people with places to serve.

An effective ministry placement process includes methods of screening and interviewing. The level of intensity of the process should be in proportion to the level of responsibility for the position. For example, churches should carefully screen individuals who will serve with children, youth, or developmentally disabled adults. Reference checks and interviews should be conducted on those who are being considered for major leadership roles. Conversely, in-depth interviews and background checks are not normally called for when placing people on usher or greeter teams. In those situations, you will likely need only to be sure candidates are friendly and can be counted on to show up when scheduled to serve.

If an interview is warranted, the interviewer should prepare a list of questions in advance. Good questions determine motivational fit, past behavior, and the likelihood of future success. "Motivational fit" questions help identify the "motives" of the candidates for seeking the ministry position. Why do they want to serve? They also help determine the level of support that candidates have for the vision and mission of the ministry and church. Past behavior questions examine experience, gifting, talents, and education. Situational questions are ones that provide scenarios likely to be encountered while serving in the position, and that evaluate the level of success candidates may have in handling them.

Once an individual is placed in a service role, follow up should be done within the first three months to ensure a good "fit." There are times when a volunteer discovers the service role isn't exactly what he or she expected. A conversation between the volunteer and a leader may yield a better match for service. The more your church can develop a reputation for putting people first through timely follow up and an effective placement service, the more eager people will be to step forward to volunteer. Don't waste opportunities to connect the people who respond to your invitation to serve!

Step 3: Equip

You have been successful in your efforts to invite and connect volunteers. Step 3 now answers this question: *What support will volunteers experience in ministry?* To equip a volunteer for service is to provide the initial and ongoing support, training, and resources needed to be effective. It is literally doing all you can to "set volunteers up for success." Have you ever been asked to do something, and then not received any support? No one told you the rules, trained you for the job, or provided feedback once you started. It's not a good feeling. People want to feel competent when serving—especially when serving God. Remember, a team environment is the most optimal, supportive environment in which to serve. Let's begin our overview of Step 3 with a look at volunteer training and resources.

Initial Training and Resources

Give thought to the volunteer position. What does the volunteer need to know in order to do the job? What equipment or other resources are needed? Depending upon the number of volunteers in a given position, it may make sense to hold a group training session. If a small number of volunteers is involved, it may make more sense to have them "shadow" existing volunteers until they are comfortable serving on their own. Be sure every volunteer knows whom to approach for help.

Ongoing Feedback and Training

Oftentimes we do not know what "equipping" skills we lack until we are actually serving in a ministry position. Check in with the volunteers serving under your care and direction. Provide them with timely feedback, praising them when things go well and guiding them when they have questions.

As a servant-leader, it is your role to search for opportunities to develop the skills you and your volunteers may need. Teams that learn together, grow together. Consider attending classes as a group at other churches that may be offering skill and leadership enhancing workshops. Depending on needs, team members may decide to attend workshops together or separately, sharing insights and materials at future team meetings. Continually watch for opportunities for growth in the church and community.

Your team also may benefit from reading books together. Different team members can lead discussions on the chapters read between meetings. Look for topics that apply to a learning or development need, or read books written by experts in the same ministry field.

Personal and Spiritual Development

View time spent together as an opportunity to minister to one another. Begin and end every gathering in prayer. Pray for one another's personal needs, as well as for your ministry work and the church. Include Bible studies or devotions in your meetings on a regular basis. Encourage one another, and hold one another accountable to commitments made to the team. A good question to ask team members occasionally is, "How is your soul?"

Coaching

Servant-leaders often assume coaching responsibilities. With coaching, the focus is on the long-term leadership development of people. Coaches create opportunities for others to "get in the game." In other words, a coach does not actually execute the plays, but enables the players to do so. Character attributes of a good coach include genuine care for and belief in people, a willingness to take a risk with potential leaders, and eagerness to develop leaders who just might be better than the coach. They celebrate the accomplishments of others and invest a lot of time and energy in helping them develop as leaders and people.

Training Your Replacement

Servant-leaders should be about the business of identifying and training their replacements. Put another way, leaders reproduce leaders. Challenge yourself and members of your team to apprentice a potential leader. Not only will this allow for the multiplication of ministry and ministers, but it also will protect the team and ministry from loss of productivity in the event that existing team members step away.

Refer back to the "Inviting People into Ministry" section of this chapter. Use the outlined steps to identify and invite a potential apprentice. Once the apprentice accepts, begin the process of progressively moving through a series of development activities. At the beginning of the process, the apprentice will simply observe you in the act of service, asking you questions from time to time. You will progress to the stage where you work in partnership, serving together. When the apprentice feels comfortable, he or she will "solo" with you standing behind-the-scenes, observing. This time you will initiate discussion about the work, providing encouragement and guidance. Finally, you will be able to release the apprentice to his or her own place of ministry. This is an effective way to grow leadership in your church.

Throughout the process of training your replacement, the apprentice will need from you your time, encouragement, and care. As you work together, you will establish trust and security for the apprentice in his or her new role. Remember to support and affirm the apprentice throughout the equipping process.

Basic Training for New and Emerging Leaders

Be on the lookout for the next generation of servant-leaders. Who are the people who should take the next leadership training class? Who might be ready for and benefit from *Leadership from the Heart*? Begin to pray about those people you will refer for leadership development on behalf of your ministry and church.

Step 4: Sustain

It is time to move on to perhaps the most challenging step in the four-step process: sustain. Think about your own life. Do you tend to focus on the needs of others first and find there is little or no time left at the end of the day to care for yourself? It's no different in ministry. Churches can be famous when it comes to burning out volunteers. It's not because the church does not care about its members. It has more to do with the fact that we are under constant pressure to meet needs and fill volunteer slots within short time constraints. Intentional planning and effort must be built into a holistic volunteer management process in order to sustain people who serve in the church.

Even Jesus took time away from the hustle and bustle of ministry to renew. He would draw away to a quiet place to pray or spend time alone with his Father. Renewal practices were in place in the Acts 2 church as people broke bread together and spent time in fellowship with one another.

Because we experience a chaotic pace in our lives outside the church, we must work extra hard to provide times of renewal within our walls. We should be preparing ourselves and the people of our churches to be in service over a lifetime—not just for a quick sprint. Let's look at a few ways we can work toward that aim.

Create a Climate of Encouragement through Recognition and Celebration

Many ministry teams have big dreams and establish audacious goals. Because people become discouraged when they look at how far they have yet to go without ever pausing to see how far they have come, it is important to recognize the small accomplishments along the way. Find ways to celebrate the incremental advances made by the team. For example, take time at monthly meetings to include ministry celebrations. Ask a question such as, "Where have you seen God working since we last met?" Even the smallest accomplishments should be cause for rejoicing.

In addition to spotlighting the accomplishments of the *team*, create a climate in which the accomplishments of *individuals* are recognized and celebrated. Recognition can take many forms, but it is best when it is sincere and personal. Be creative. You do not need to have a large budget to find meaningful ways to say "thank you." Some leaders pass out candy "hugs" or "kudos" bars to encourage their volunteers. Others write personal notes that include details of how a person's service impacted individual lives or contributed to the vision of the church. If possible, have the people who benefit from the service of the volunteer write a note of thanks. Celebrate milestones outside of ministry, too, such as weddings, births, graduations, and promotions.

Take Time for Reflection and Evaluation

Provide time occasionally for volunteers to reflect on their works of service. This can be done informally and in a short amount of time. Ask questions such as these: Where did you sense God working today? How did our service fulfill the purpose of the church? How did our work impact you personally? It sustains people when they see the impact their service has on the lives of other people, the community, and the church.

In addition, take time annually to conduct a one-on-one evaluation with every person to whom you provide leadership. Allow the person to reflect on his or her ministry contribution, share stories, and evaluate the current service role in light of present life circumstances. This is a time for the individual either to recommit to the same ministry position, move on to another role, or perhaps take a break. Pray with and for the person. If the decision is to move on, help to plan a smooth transition, even offering to help make a connection with another ministry area leader.

A team should evaluate its effectiveness annually, as well. Evaluation questions should measure understanding and commitment to the mission statement, elements of community within the team, effectiveness of service, collaboration amongst team members and with other ministries, and the growth and development of team members. (A sample evaluation can be found on the resource DVD.)

Plan Renewal Events and Retreats

Church-wide gatherings for the purpose of celebration and renewal are one way to sustain your committed volunteers. For example, every January, servant-leaders at The Church of the Resurrection have an opportunity to be renewed and refreshed at an event called *The Summit*. In addition to training workshops, *The Summit* agenda includes Christian fellowship, intimate worship and communion, and a time of anointing. The senior pastor shares a word of encouragement and inspires those gathered with God's vision for the church in the coming year. Past ministry milestones are celebrated. Events such as this are wonderful ways to refresh and rejuvenate a ministry team.

Annual team retreats are beneficial, as well, and can be planned for minimal cost. Most denominations have nearby camps that can be rented out by groups. Generally, they are located in areas where people can spend time enjoying nature. Simple, yet meaningful, retreats can be planned right at your own church with a little effort and creativity. Some of your church members might have homes that would be conducive to a retreat, especially if there are no longer small children in the home.

If you are able to retreat as a team, be sure to build in quiet time for personal reflection, worship, and other spiritual renewal activities, as well as plenty of Christian fellowship. It is okay to attend to business, but remember that if there is too much business, it will cease to be a "retreat."

Conclusion

You have considered four steps to holistic volunteer management. The steps are simple in theory, yet can be hard to put into practice. Do not be overwhelmed. Start by making a baby step in each of the four areas. If you look at your church's current approach toward volunteers, you will find areas where your church is already doing quite well. Help your church to focus first on developing the areas where it has the most potential for growth.

You might also want to type on a sheet of paper the actual words—invite, connect, equip, sustain—and evaluate how you are doing personally in each of the four areas as you develop as a servant-leader. At any given time, you will find you are doing better at some steps than others. Work with your team to bring balance to its efforts to holistically prepare people to serve.

Biblical Foundation

As you review each Scripture passage, underline or circle key words or phrases. Think about the implications of each passage for your life, noting your insights in the space provided. Answer the questions that follow.

Indeed the body does not consist of one member, but of many. If the foot would say, "Because I am not a hand, I do not belong to the body," that would not make it any less a part of the body. And if the ear would say, "Because I am not an eye, I do not belong to the body," that would not make it any less a part of the body. If the whole body were an eye, where would the hearing be? If the whole body were hearing, where would the sense of smell be? But as it is, God arranged the members in the body, each one of them, as he chose. If all

were a single member, where would the body be? As it is, there are many parts, yet one body. (1 Corinthians 12:14-20)

As [Jesus] walked by the Sea of Galilee, he saw two brothers, Simon, who is called Peter, and Andrew his brother, casting a net into the sea—for they were fishermen. And he said to them, "Follow me, and I will make you fish for people." Immediately they left their nets and followed him. As he went from there, he saw two other brothers, James son of Zebedee and his brother John, in the boat with their father Zebedee, mending their nets, and he called them. Immediately they left the boat and their father and followed him. (Matthew 4:18-22)

Then Jesus called the twelve together and gave them power and authority over all demons and to cure diseases, and he sent them out to proclaim the kingdom of God and heal. (Luke 9:1-2 NIV)

As the Father has loved me, so I have loved you; abide in my love. If you keep my commandments, you will abide in my love, just as I have kept my Father's commandments and abide in his love. I have said these things to you so that my joy may be in you and that your joy may be complete. This is my commandment, that you love one another as I have loved you. No one has greater love than this, to lay down one's life for one's friends. You are my friends if you do what I command you. I do not call you servants any longer, because the servant does not know what the master is doing; but I have called you friends, because I have made known to you everything that I have heard from my Father. You did not choose me, but I chose you. And I appointed you to go and bear fruit, fruit that will last, so that the Father will give you whatever you ask him in my name. I am giving

you these commands so that you may love one another. (John 15:9-17)

Now during those days, when the disciples were increasing in number, the Hellenists among them complained against the Hebrews because their widows were being neglected in the daily distribution of food. And the twelve called together the whole community of the disciples and said, "It is not right that we should neglect the word of God in order to wait on tables. Therefore friends, select from among yourselves seven men of good standing, full of the Spirit and of wisdom, whom we may appoint to this task, while we, for our part, devote ourselves to prayer and to serving the word." What they said pleased the whole community, and they chose Stephen, a man full of faith and the Holy Spirit; together with Philip, Procorus, Nicanor, Timon, Parmenas, and Nicholas, a proselyte of Antioch. They had these men stand before the apostles, who prayed and laid their hands on them. The word of God continued to spread; the number of the disciples increased greatly in Jerusalem, and a great many of priests became obedient to the faith. (Acts 6:1-7)

As God's chosen ones, holy and beloved, clothe yourselves with compassion, kindness, humility, meekness and patience. Bear with one another and, if anyone has a complaint against another, forgive each other; just as the Lord forgave you, so you also must forgive. Above all, clothe yourselves with love, which binds everything together in perfect harmony. And let the peace of Christ rule in your hearts, to which indeed you were called in the one body. And be thankful. Let the word of Christ dwell in you richly; teach and admonish one another in all wisdom; and with gratitude in your hearts sing psalms, hymns, and spiritual songs to God. And whatever you do, in word or deed, do everything in the name of the Lord Jesus, giving thanks to God the Father through him. (Colossians 3:12-17)

Reflection Questions

1. What does the passage from 1 Corinthians 12 mean in terms of your role as a servant-leader? What does it say about the roles of others in your church?

2. It is believed that Andrew and Peter already knew Jesus when he called them to follow him in Matthew 4 (see John 1:35-42). What about their knowledge of Jesus and his mission might have compelled Andrew and Peter, as well as James and John, to leave their businesses and families to follow Jesus? What does this imply for a leader who invites others to join his or her ministry team?

3. What equipping concepts does Jesus model in Luke 9:1-2?

4. Describe Jesus' relationship with his team, the disciples, in John 15. What does this say about our attitudes and actions toward those with whom we serve?

5. What volunteer management strategies did the apostles employ in Acts 6:1-6? What were the results described in verse 7?

6. According to Colossians 3, what might be a good recipe for building unity among people who serve in the church together?

 # HEART

Taking It to Heart

1. Describe the heart and actions of a servant-leader who invited you into ministry, connected you with a role to fit your gifts, effectively equipped you, and provided the means to sustain you as you served. If you cannot think of an example from church, try to think of a supervisor, coach, parent or teacher—someone who prepared you for a new challenge.

2. Describe any experience(s) you have had in inviting, connecting, equipping, and/or sustaining the work of another. Feel free to use examples outside the church.

3. What do you do to sustain yourself and your ministry? What might you do that you are not already doing?

Heart to Heart

1. As a group, develop a two- to three-sentence summary of the video presentation.

2. Discuss the Scripture passages from this week's reading. Several of the passages address situations where the work of ministry was not done until others were invited to serve. Discuss the implications of this to ministry, then and now.

3. Discuss your thoughts, ideas, and experiences relating to each of the four volunteer-management steps:

   Invite

   Connect

   Equip

   Sustain

4. Take five minutes individually to develop a 30-second commercial for any ministry in which you have served, or currently serve. Take turns sharing your commercials.

 HANDS

Action Plan

1. With your accountability partner(s), share your conclusions about the effective team you chose. Discuss the goal you have set to implement one of the successful team-building steps in your own ministry.

2. Over the next week, create a list of the best volunteer management practices you see at work in your church. You will likely find that some ministries excel at one or more of the four steps, but not all of them. Write out some ideas you have for ways in which the ministry areas within your church might learn from one another's best practices.

3. Find a tangible, measurable way to practice at least one concept you have learned from this chapter. For example, you might choose to identify one individual to personally invite or refer to your church's next leadership study or training course. Briefly share with your accountability partner(s) the concept you chose, along with your plan for implementation. Write your action plan in the space provided, including the names of any individuals in whom you plan to invest your time, knowledge, energy, and love. Be prepared next week to share any steps you have taken or progress you have made.

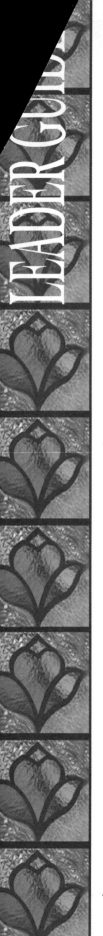

LEADER GUIDE

SESSION 10

LEADING FROM THE HEART

Caring for the People We Lead

Materials Needed:

◆ nametags
◆ pens or pencils
◆ TV and DVD player

For opening activity:
◆ Index cards, enough for each participant to have one for every member of his or her small group.

Room Set-up:

◆ Arrange pre-assigned groups around tables so that members are facing one another.
◆ Place TV and DVD player so that all can see (participants may need to turn their chairs around to view video).

Timing:

This outline is designed to cover a ninety-minute session. If you prefer to fit this into a sixty-minute format, we suggest deleting the Opening Activity and reducing the Heart to Heart Small Group Discussion to thirty minutes and the Hands Action Plan to ten minutes. If you prefer a two-hour format, include a fifteen-minute break after the Video Presentation Discussion, and add fifteen minutes to the Heart to Heart Small Group Discussion.

Opening Prayer and Welcome

(5 minutes)

Welcome participants to *Leadership from the Heart*, Session 10. The purpose of this session is to gain understanding of how we are to care for and nurture those we lead.

Opening Activity

(30 minutes)

The purpose of this activity is to allow participants to feel encouraged and affirmed. Understanding how it feels to be affirmed will help them grasp how the people they lead feel when they receive affirmation or encouragement.

The small group guide should select someone in the group to be the first to receive "affirmation," and lead off by reading what he or she has written on an index card for this person. Then the guide may present the card to the person receiving the affirmation. Next the group members take turns around the table, with each participant repeating the process until all members have "affirmed" that recipient. Continue until all participants have received affirmation. Allow twenty-five minutes for this activity.

Use the following questions to generate a short discussion:

1. How did it feel to be affirmed and encouraged in this way?
2. What insights did you glean from this activity?
3. How can you affirm and encourage those you lead?

Video Presentation

Rob Winger (Approx. 15 minutes)

Play the video segment for Session 10.

Full Group Video Discussion

(5 minutes)

Facilitate a full group discussion based on the video presentation using the questions that follow. Don't be nervous if no one responds immediately. If there is a pause and you do not fill in the silence, someone eventually will speak up! After someone responds, ask for other comments. After one or two comments, go on to the next question, and so forth. Try to keep this initial discussion brief and to the point. Inform the participants that more in-depth discussion will follow in their small groups.

1. Sometimes we are intimidated at the thought of providing pastoral care for others What are we so afraid of? Are those fears valid?
2. The speaker pointed out that Jesus often criticized the religious leaders of his day for being so focused on doing things "right" that they neglected doing the "right" thing— having compassion for the people they were called to lead. We sometimes fall into the same trap. How can we avoid that?
3. What other insights did you glean from the video?

Bring the group back to this key point:
As we build relationships with the people we lead, we become, in many ways, the most appropriate person to provide a measure of pastoral care when they have needs. In most cases, it's not about knowing the right things to say; it's just about "being there."

Heart to Heart Small Group Discussions

(20 minutes)

Each small group guide should start the discussion by reminding group members that the discussion questions are not designed to have "right" or "wrong" answers. They are meant to encourage group members to share their own insights and experiences, as well as what they've learned, so that members of the group can learn from one another. Everyone has something to offer! The guide should encourage each person to participate, and should keep any one individual from dominating the discussion. Refer to the Tips for Small Group Guides in this *Leader's Guide* (page 8) for pointers on group facilitation.

Begin by asking the group to summarize the video presentation. Groups should try to get that message into a few short sentences.

Ask group members which passage(s) from this week's Scripture spoke to them and why.

Continue the discussion using the Heart to Heart questions on page 126.

Hands Action Plan

(15 minutes)

Small group guides should direct group members to get with their accountability partner(s) and proceed with the Hands portion of the session on page 126.

First, they each take one minute reporting their progress on last week's action plan. What did and did not happen as they had hoped?

Next, they take six to eight minutes developing their action plans for this week.

Finally, each one shares his or her action plan for the upcoming week.

Closing Circle Prayer

(5 minutes)

Small group guides should bring the accountability partners of the small groups back together for joys and concerns and a closing prayer. Ask the participants to keep their comments brief, encouraging them to share detailed prayer requests outside of class time— either in person, on the phone, or via e-mail.

We encourage you to use a circle prayer format to close the small group time. The ability to lead a group in prayer is essential in Christian leadership, but many people are not comfortable praying aloud. Circle prayers are useful in helping people become comfortable praying in a group. Remind the participants that their words do not have to be elaborate— just from the heart!

Have members stand, if they are able, holding hands around the table. Ask each person to speak one sentence in prayer, with the small group guide opening and closing the prayer.

CHAPTER 10

LEADING FROM THE HEART

Caring for the People We Lead

"Come to me, all you who are weary and burdened, and I will give you rest. Take my yoke upon you and learn from me, for I am gentle and humble in heart, and you will find rest for your souls. For my yoke is easy and my burden is light."
(Matthew 11:28-30)

 **HEAD**

Key Insights

◆ Jesus cares far more about how we treat the people he has entrusted to our care than how "productive" we are.

◆ Servant-leaders are loving and compassionate shepherds, following the example of The Good Shepherd, Jesus Christ. Like Jesus, we must have hearts that beat for lost and hurting people.

◆ We must develop an awareness of what is and is not within our scope of care.

◆ Looking to God for guidance and strength and practicing self-care is essential to our ability to care for others.

Understanding the Concept

A common challenge facing many churches today is providing quality pastoral care to all of their members. We have fallen into the trap of believing that the ministry of care belongs solely to ordained clergy. Though there are some areas that remain the domain of the ordained, depending on each denomination's guidelines, there are many needs that can be met by caring members of the laity. Servant-leaders play an important role in providing and modeling shepherding to the people with whom they interact on a regular basis.

Jesus demonstrated the importance of caring for others. His heart beat for people, and he took the time to listen and care for those around him. Jesus' heart also beat with love for his Father. When the rigors of ministry depleted him, he withdrew to spend time in the presence of his Father to be replenished and renewed. We can learn from his example to better care for others as well as ourselves. Self-care is equally important because, without it, even the most gifted and caring servant-leader will run the risk of burn-out.

Tend Your Sheep

Providing care can be compared to tending sheep. Both the Old and New Testaments are filled with the imagery of shepherds and sheep. David was a shepherd when God called him to be king. Jacob and Moses tended sheep as well. When God spoke through the prophets Isaiah, Jeremiah, and Ezekiel, he utilized the metaphor of shepherds tending sheep. Jesus taught using the same metaphor, often describing himself as the Good Shepherd. He later admonished Peter to feed his lambs and sheep and to take care of his sheep. Paul and Peter challenged the elders and overseers of the early churches to be good shepherds of the flocks under their care.

Though we may not have firsthand knowledge of the intricacies in the relationship between the shepherd and his sheep, this would have been readily understood by people in biblical times, for it was an important element of their culture. We can, however, glean enough information about this relationship from Scripture to apply it to our own leadership. As we will learn together, the shepherd/sheep relationship is one that is both personal and hands-on in nature. Sheep learn to trust the shepherd, and the shepherd is committed and available to the individual members of the flock. The Hebrew word for shepherd, used in many Old Testament passages, is *râ'âh*, which translates to *tend* a flock; pasture it; to associate with (as a friend); companion, keep company with, make friendship with. The Greek word for shepherd is *pŏimēn*, which also means pastor. *Webster's New World Dictionary's* definition of the word *care* includes the following: to feel concern; to look after; provide (for). We might define *pastoral care*, then, as a pastor or shepherd being concerned with, looking after, and/or providing for the needs of people, with a spiritual touch.

Perhaps you have never considered yourself a shepherd of any sheep. You may see that as the role of the pastor, or pastors, of the church. This is true—God has appointed our pastors to be shepherds over his flock—our congregation. He also has gifted and empowered each one of us to serve as shepherds of much smaller flocks within the larger congregation. These include members of our ministry teams and small groups—those people with whom the servant-leader interacts on an ongoing basis. Consider these words of Robert Slocum in his book *Maximize Your Ministry*:

> The effective church for the twenty-first century will be the church that mobilizes, equips, empowers and supports *ordinary Christians* in ministry. By *ordinary Christians*, I mean the laity, the lay men and women who are not church professionals, yet who make up more than 98 percent of the people of God. It is of critical importance for us *ordinary Christians* to understand who we are, what we are supposed to do and where we are supposed to do it. ([Colorado Springs, CO: Navpress, 1990] p. 7-8)

If ordinary Christians make up 98 percent of God's people and ordained clergy make up the other 2 percent, how well do you think it will work to have only 2 percent of God's people provide pastoral care to the other 98 percent? Consider the example of a 10,000 member church with six ordained clergy on the staff. Three of these pastors have vast duties outside the pastoral care arena. Even if all six were available full-time to provide pastoral care, it would mean that each would be responsible for over 1,650 members! That is definitely not God's plan. Fortunately, many pastors today have rediscovered God's plan for pastoral care—which began with Moses—and are equipping the lay people of their churches to meet basic pastoral care needs. Many churches are training Stephen Ministers, lay hospital callers, and even lay pastors. Above and beyond these and other programs, "ordinary" church members are taking it upon themselves to provide encouragement and care to the people in their small groups and ministry service teams.

What does this mean for us as leaders? How might we shepherd the flocks under our care? Let's start by looking at some very practical ways we can provide pastoral care.

1. Build Community

Community is the "glue" that cements groups together. In order for real community to be established, there must be an overall atmosphere of genuine Christian fellowship. As servant-leaders, we can help cultivate this atmosphere of fellowship by building relationships with and between the members of our small communities—people on our ministry teams or in our small groups. We must remember, however, that this takes both time and intentionality. We cannot "microwave" the process.

Sheep come to know and trust the voice of their shepherd over time. This level of intimacy develops because the shepherd spends time with the sheep as a hands-on caretaker. Likewise, as we build relationships with the people we lead, we are better positioned not only to *provide* care to them, but also to *receive* care from them. Trust develops and spirits are nurtured. As an added benefit, we are more effective in our role as leader. As the relationship leader and follower deepens, the [...]ness of the follower to be led grows. People [...]uch more willing to follow someone who [...]entically cares for them.

We have seen this type of fellowship modeled by [...] leadership team that sponsors national training events each year. Their motto is "eat, drink, play, and pray together." And, they do! They also work together, encourage one another, and provide tangible support to one another. During a training event several years ago, the team director's daughter became ill back home. Members of the team encouraged her to leave the conference, assuring her they would work together to cover her training and leadership responsibilities. The event was seamless to the outside observer. This highly successful ministry team has never lost sight of their calling to first care for one another; relationships come before tasks with this group.

One of the best ways to build relationships is to plan regular times for group and individual sharing. Some groups have regular "check-in" time at team meetings so that team members can "catch up" with one another on a personal level—learn what's going on with family and friends or at their workplaces. Other teams provide refreshments and a fellowship break. Healthy teams also plan gatherings outside of the regular meeting schedule just to socialize or play, such as movie nights or attending a baseball game.

As we discussed in a previous chapter, one of the best tools for laying a foundation of fellowship is to formulate a team covenant. In signing a covenant, group members agree to hold themselves and one another accountable to agreed-upon values such as acceptance, commitment, honesty, confidentiality, and humility. These values protect the dignity of individuals and help establish an atmosphere of trust, which is essential to authentic community. (A sample covenant can be found on the resource DVD.)

Jesus modeled these values as a humble servant-leader. As servant-leaders, we also must adopt an attitude of humility. This involves taking the focus off of ourselves and becoming responsive to the needs of others. We must be careful, however, that we do not offer false humility or begin to view ourselves as martyrs. This is why it is important to be in a place where we are experiencing the love of Jesus on a regular basis through prayer, study, and Christian fellowship. Christ-like humility develops as we deepen our relationship with Jesus; it is a by-product of our spiritual growth. As humble servant-leaders, we put others first and earn the trust of our followers. Fellowship thrives as those we lead feel genuinely welcomed and unconditionally accepted.

2. Provide Spiritual Nurture

In John 21, Jesus commands Peter to feed his lambs and sheep. Shepherds provide spiritual nurture to those in their care. They are concerned with the spiritual growth of those they lead. It is easy to get caught up in the demands of ministry or the task at hand. Though we are meant to serve, service should not come at the expense of losing our souls. There are simple steps we can take to enhance spiritual nurture—of others and ourselves:

◆ Prayer should be at the center of every ministry. Begin and end time together with prayer. Take time to share personal joys and concerns, and covenant to pray for one another when team members are not together.

◆ Incorporate Bible study into the agenda. Sometimes this may have to take the form of a simple devotion. When time allows, perhaps in a retreat setting, the group can do a more in-depth study. Relate what you are studying to the ministry you are doing whenever possible.

◆ Check in with individual team members from time-to-time and ask them about their spiritual growth. We are prone to asking the question, "How are you?" What about asking instead, "How is your soul?"

3. Listen

One of the greatest gifts we can give another human being is our listening ear. Listening to another person is an active pursuit. It involves giving the speaker our full attention, stopping all other activity in which we are currently engaged, and exhibiting attentiveness with our body language. It also means listening beyond the actual words being spoken, searching for deeper or hidden meaning. People are prone to say with their words that everything is okay when their eyes and overall demeanor say the complete opposite.

If you are a parent, you can relate to this phenomenon. Your son or daughter comes home from school looking visibly upset. When you ask your child what's wrong, the answer is usually *"Nothing."* So, you must stick with the conversation and probe a little further to get your child to open up and share. Often what your child shares comes out in bits and pieces, requiring time and effort to really listen for the actual problem and get to the heart of the matter. Too often, we miss the meaning behind what is being said because we do not listen in this manner.

When we do listen attentively, we sometimes are too quick to offer advice—to attempt to fix the person or problem when what might be needed is sympathy. Sympathy is essentially seeing a situation from another's point of view and sharing his or her pain. As numerous experts have observed, it meets the basic human need to be understood and have our feelings affirmed. Offering sympathy takes time in our oft-hurried lives. Again, we can look to Jesus as our example. He demonstrated compassion for people every time he stopped to minister to their needs. Jesus was open to having his agenda changed, and he did so in a way that never deterred from his mission. Listening with our hearts is a simple way we can provide pastoral care.

> **"Compassion means to become close to the one who suffers. But we can come close to another person only when we are willing to be vulnerable ourselves. A compassionate person says: "I am your brother; I am your sister; I am human, fragile, and mortal, just like you. I am not scandalized by your tears, nor afraid of your pain. I too have wept. I too have felt pain." We can be with the other only when the other ceases to be other and becomes like us."**
>
> ~Henri Nouwen

One word of caution: Though it is helpful to validate a person's feelings in most situations we encounter—such as grief over the death of a loved one—there are times when we should not affirm the feelings of others. We need not listen to gossip or affirm conflicts in the church, in a particular ministry, or with a particular person. Trust your instincts and the guidance of the Holy Spirit.

4. Provide Practical Help and Practice Random Acts of Kindness

Shepherding also can take the form of simple, personal, everyday tasks performed from the heart. This kind of caring occurred in the church of the early believers, as we read in Acts 2:42-47. The Apostle Paul sometimes mentioned the practical care he received in the closing sentences of his letters. Here are a few examples we might follow:

◆ Sending cards or notes of encouragement or thanks.
◆ Taking a meal to someone just home from the hospital.
◆ Attending the funeral of a team member's loved one.
◆ Watching someone's children while they visit the doctor.
◆ Raking the leaves or mowing the lawn of someone who is ill.
◆ Inviting a person in need of encouragement out for a cup of coffee.
◆ Making an encouraging phone call—even praying over the phone.
◆ Visiting a group member in the hospital.
◆ Running errands for someone unable to drive.
◆ Use your imagination—the list could go on and on…

...n overlook the simple ideas, and yet they ...ey a great deal of thoughtful caring.

What Is Within Your Scope of Care

...ne of the most important tasks we have related ...tending our sheep" is developing an awareness of ...hat is and is not within our scope of care. In other words, there will be times when a need is beyond the scope of what we are equipped to handle. At times we can better serve individuals by helping them to connect with a pastor, professional counselor, support group, or trained Stephen Minister. As leaders, we must educate ourselves with the knowledge of available resources. Most churches maintain a contact list of support groups, counselors, agencies, and ministry programs that provide specific forms of care. When in doubt, always ask for guidance.

Remember, also, that sheep must be willing and committed to following the shepherd. We cannot force care on an individual. As you continue to develop as a servant-leader, your sensitivity to the appropriateness of your care for others will develop. Err on the side of caution. When in doubt, ask a pastor or other trusted and proven leader in the church for guidance. It is also strongly recommended you provide more intimate forms of pastoral care—those involving one-to-one contact—to members of the same gender. In this way, you avoid putting yourself, or the other person, in a compromising position, especially when the person is most vulnerable. An individual experiencing a serious personal crisis may rely heavily upon the person providing care. Even listening to the concerns and feelings of a member of the opposite sex can send confusing signals. Trust that you and the other party will be better served by asking the question, *Who is the best person to provide care in this situation?*

Look to God for Guidance and Strength

Finally, in order for us to be good and faithful shepherds of the flocks entrusted to our care, we must model a healthy ministry by constantly looking to our Good Shepherd for guidance and strength. Jesus does not expect us to care for people absent of his care and protection. He invites us to take upon ourselves his yoke, which is not burdensome. He has promised to "be with us always" and has empowered us for ministry through the indwelling of the Holy Spirit.

We cannot give what we do not have, which is why we must not let our wells run dry. When we allow ourselves to become spiritually or emotionally deprived and malnourished, we quickly become overwhelmed by the needs of others, and it eventually impacts others serving with us. God knows our limitations and desires that we turn to him for provision. In the account of the feeding of the five thousand found in Matthew 14, the disciples wanted Jesus to dismiss the crowd so that the people could get something to eat. Jesus' response to the disciples was to suggest they feed the people. The disciples were overwhelmed at the thought—they were operating from a mindset of scarcity. Jesus asked the disciples to give him everything they had, and they produced five loaves and two fish. Close your eyes for a moment and try to picture the faces of the disciples. Can you imagine what must have been going through their minds?

The story does not end there. Jesus took everything he had, lifted it to the Father, and gave thanks. Miraculously, the five loaves and two fish fed five thousand men, plus hungry women and children, and there were twelve basketsful of leftovers—one for each of the disciples. Perhaps this story is in the Bible to remind us that God knows everything we have to offer. He asks us simply to turn it over to him and trust him to multiply our resources to meet the need at hand. In order to do this, we must operate from a mindset of abundance.

How do we achieve this mindset? *We take care of ourselves.* Be diligent in caring for your own health—physical, emotional, mental, and spiritual. Exercise, rest, and maintain a healthy diet. Spend time with your closest loved ones and social time with friends, nurturing the important relationships in your life. Continue to grow in knowledge, stretching your mind. Be consistent in your prayer and Bible study. Your participation in this study is evidence that you are already building your leadership on a solid spiritual foundation. Continue to practice the spiritual disciplines for renewal, invest in your own development, and plan regular times of rest and refreshment.

As we learned in a previous chapter, we draw spiritual nourishment when we, as branches, remain in the vine, which represents Jesus (see John 15). Branches that are removed from the vine wither and die. This is a graphic but true illustration. The shepherd cannot feed his or her sheep when suffering from starvation. If we attempt to meet the needs of others utilizing our own strength and resources, we will quickly find ourselves completely depleted.

Remember, also, that God has entrusted *our* care to others—pastors and other leaders in the church—whose responsibility it is to teach and care for *us*. Even pastors need such care. They, too, are human beings, not super-heroes. God desires to provide for the care needs of all his children. If you are not receiving the care you need, seek it out. Always remember: Ministry is a marathon, not a sprint. God loves you and desires for you to be available for the long haul.

Biblical Foundation

As you review each Scripture passage, underline or circle key words or phrases. Think about the implications of each passage for your life, noting your insights in the space provided. Answer the questions that follow.

For thus says the LORD GOD: "I myself will search for my sheep and will seek them out. As shepherds seek out their flocks when they are among their scattered sheep, so I will seek out my sheep. I will rescue them from all the places to which they have been scattered on a day of clouds and thick darkness. I will bring them out from the peoples and gather them from the countries, and will bring them into their own land; and I will feed them on the mountains of Israel, by the watercourses, and in all the inhabited parts of the land. I will feed them with good pasture, and the mountain heights of Israel shall be their pasture; there they shall lie down in good grazing land, and there they shall feed on rich pasture on the mountains of Israel. I myself will be the shepherd of my sheep, and I will make them lie down, says the Lord GOD. I will seek the lost, and I will bring back the strayed,

and I will bind up the injured, and I will strengthen the weak, but the fat and the strong I will destroy. I will feed them with justice." (Ezekiel 34:11-16)

[Jesus said,] "I am the good shepherd. The good shepherd lays down his life for the sheep. The hired hand, who is not the shepherd and does not own the sheep, sees the wolf coming and leaves the sheep and runs away—and the wolf snatches them and scatters them. The hired hand runs away because a hired hand does not care for the sheep. I am the good shepherd. I know my own and my own know me, just as the Father knows me and I know the Father. And I lay down my life for the sheep. I have other sheep that do not belong to this fold. I must bring them also, and they will listen to my voice. So there will be one flock, one shepherd." (John 10:11-16)

When they had finished breakfast, Jesus said to Simon Peter, "Simon son of John, do you love me more than these?" He said to him, "Yes, Lord: you know I that I love you." Jesus said to him "Feed my lambs." A second time he said to him, "Simon son of John, do you love me?" He said to him, "Yes, Lord, you know that I love you." Jesus said to him, "Tend my sheep." He said to him the third time, "Simon, son of John, do you love me?" Peter felt hurt because he said to him the third time, "Do you love me?" And he said to him, "Lord, you know everything; you know that I love you." Jesus said to him "Feed my sheep." (John 21:15-18)

When it was evening, the disciples came to him and said, "This is a deserted place the hour is now late; send the

…so that they may go into the villages and buy …mselves." Jesus said to them, "They need not go …give them something to eat." They replied, "We …hing here but five loaves and two fish. And he said, …them here to me." Then he ordered the crowds to sit …on the grass. Taking the five loaves and the two fish, …ooked up to heaven, and blessed and broke the loaves, and …ve them to the disciples, and the disciples gave them to the crowds. And all ate and were filled, and they took up what was left over of the broken pieces, twelve baskets full. And those who ate were about five thousand men, besides the women and children. (Matthew 14:15-21)

"Come to me, all you that are weary and carrying heavy burdens, and I will give you rest. Take my yoke upon you and learn from me, for I am gentle and humble in heart, and you will find rest for your souls. For my yoke is easy and my burden is light." (Matthew 11:28-30)

Now as an elder myself and a witness of the sufferings of Christ, as well as one who also shares in the glory to be revealed, I exhort the elders among you to tend the flock of God that is in your charge, exercising the oversight, not under compulsion but willingly, as God would have you do it—not for sordid gain but eagerly. Do not lord it over those in your charge, but being examples to the flock. And when the Chief Shepherd appears, you will win the crown of glory that never fades away. (1 Peter 5:1-4)

Read devotionally and reflect upon each line of Psalm 23 individually. What do these words of promise mean to you personally? Write out your thoughts in the spaces provided, line by line.

The LORD is my shepherd, I shall not want,

He makes me lie down in green pastures,

He leads me beside still waters,

He restores my soul.

He leads me in right paths for his name's sake.

Even though I walk through the darkest valley,

I fear no evil, for you are with me;

Your rod and your staff, they comfort me.

You prepare a table before me in the presence of my enemies.

You anoint my head with oil;

My cup overflows.

Surely goodness and mercy shall follow me all the days of my life,

and I shall dwell in the house of the LORD my whole life long. (Psalm 23)

Reflection Questions

1. In Ezekiel 34, God spoke out against the shepherds of Israel for their mistreatment of the flock and, beginning at verse 11, promised to shepherd the flock himself. How would you characterize God as shepherd from the passage in Ezekiel?

2. Contrast the characteristics of the good shepherd with those of the hired hand as described in John 10. In what ways do we sometimes behave like the hired hand? The good shepherd?

3. What exactly was Jesus asking of Peter in John 21? (You may want to refer to a study Bible and concordance for deeper study; this passage is rich with meaning.) Relate this to your own role as a servant-leader for Jesus. What is Jesus asking of you?

4. Describe the attitude of the disciples toward the people in Matthew 14. What was Jesus' plan for meeting their needs? How might our perspectives regarding our limitations and God's provision affect our attitudes about meeting the needs of others?

5. There are times when every Christian feels overwhelmed by the burdens he or she carries.

What is Jesus' advice in Matthew 11, and v do you think this means? Is caring for others meant to be a burden?

6. According to 1 Peter 5, what is the role of elders and overseers in the church? How do you think this passage might apply to all church leaders — both ordained clergy and laypersons?

 # HEART

Taking It to Heart

1. Describe a situation where a layperson provided pastoral care to you. Did it bother you that this person was not an ordained pastor? Why or why not?

2. Describe an experience where you provided pastoral care to someone else. Did you feel comfortable and equipped to provide this care? If not, what would have made you feel better about the situation?

3. What must you do to do to enhance your ability and comfort level as a shepherd?

eart

roup, develop a two- to three-sentence
nary of the video presentation.

2. Discuss the Scripture passages from this week's reading. What did you learn about shepherding ministry teams from these readings?

3. Share your firsthand pastoral care experiences—both as recipient and provider—with the members of your small group.

4. Discuss and list with your group appropriate situations and ways to provide pastoral care, as well as situations when you would refer the individual to someone else.

Situation: **I could do this:**

I would ask for help with:

 # HANDS

Action Plan

1. Share with your accountability partner(s) any steps you have taken to implement your chosen concept in your own ministry.

2. Now share with your accountability partner(s) the ways you are being fed spiritually—those things that keep you from depleting your own resources for providing care to others. What can you do to improve in these areas? Write your action plan in the space provided, and briefly share with your accountability partner(s).

3. Find one person this week in need of some form of encouragement, and provide it. Try to make it as personal as possible. For example, rather than sending someone a note of encouragement, take him or her out for a cup of coffee and deliver your encouragement in person. Write about your experience in the space provided. Include details about what "being there" for someone else meant to you, how the person responded to your care efforts, and how you sensed God working throughout the experience

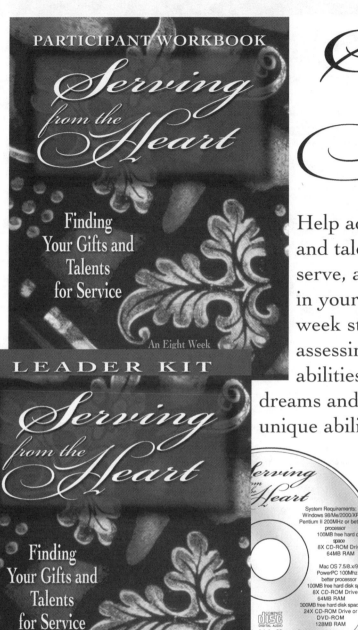

PARTICIPANT WORKBOOK

Serving from the Heart

Finding Your Gifts and Talents for Service

An Eight Week

LEADER KIT

Serving from the Heart

Finding Your Gifts and Talents for Service

CD-ROM Included

An Eight Week Study for Small Groups

Serving from the Heart

Help adults discover their unique gifts and talents for service, the insipiration to serve, and a way to connect with service in your church community. This 4-to 8-week study leads adults through assessing their spiritual gifts, talents and abilities, resources, individual style, dreams and experiences—all adding up to a unique ability to serve God and neighbor.

The leader kit includes easy to follow lesson plans for either eight 45-minute sessions or four 2-hour sessions. The enhanced CD-ROM included in the kit makes leading convenient and creative with overhead slides, posters, music and leader training video, from the ministry staff at Church of the Resurrection.

Serving from the Heart Leader Kit 0687081076 - $34.00
Serving from the Heart Participant Workbook 0687081173 - $10.00

DVD-ROM Instructions

...wing on Television

...the ten video segments for class use, place the
...in a DVD player connected to a television and
...s "Play". Choices for the ten sessions will appear.
...ct the week's session and press "Play".

For Use on Personal Computer

The presentation on this DVD should automatically start
when placed in the DVD-Rom drive of your personal
computer. If it does not start automatically:

Microsoft Windows users:

Under the START menu, locate your DVD Player
software in the list of Programs. When the DVD player
application is open, simply click the PLAY button to
initialize the DVD-Rom.

Mac OS users

Locate your DVD Player software. When the DVD
Player application is
open, simply click the PLAY button to initialize the
DVD-Rom.

Opening the Files (Mac or PC)

When DVD @cess is enabled on any Apple or PC
computer, each of the documents will automatically open
when the menu option is selected from the Resources
menu. If your machine can not perform the DVD@cess
functions, all documents are located on the DVD disk
and may be manually opened by opening the DVD within
"My Computer" and selecting the file you would like to
open.

To open the Microsoft Word document, you must have
a registered version of Microsoft Word on your
workstation. If you do not have Word, a PDF version of
the Word document has been provided. To open PDF
files, you must have Adobe PDF Reader, Adobe Acrobat,
or a PDF translator application loaded on your
workstation. This software is available free of charge on
several web sites including Cokesbury.com and the
Adobe software site.
To find this easy-to-use software, visit:
http://www.cokesbury.com/digitalstore.aspx?subSection=18
or
http://www.adobe.com/products/acrobat/readstep2.html

System Requirements

Windows 98/Me/2000/XP
Pentium II 200MHz or better processor
DVD-Rom Drive with DVD-Video player software with
DVD@cess
64MB Ram

Mac OS 9.x / 10.x
PowerPC 300 Mhz or better processor
DVD-Rom Drive with DVD-Video player software with
DVD@cess
64 MB Ram
To take advantage of the DVD-Rom features on this disk,
you must have DVD@ccess capabilities. Below are
instructions for adding this functionality to your
workstation:

APPLE/ MAC USERS

Apple's DVD Player Software:
• Open Apple's DVD player software.
• Select Disc Setup.
• Under the Internet option, select the Enable
  DVD@ccess web links check box.
• Click OK.

WINDOWS USERS

PC DVD@ccess Installer:
If you do not currently have DVD@cess functionality,
you can add it to your PC. Inside your dvd-rom, a special
folder is included called DVD@cess. Locate this folder by
right-clicking the DVD under "My Computer" and
choosing the "Explore" option. Inside this DVD@cess
folder is a dvd access enabler for PC users as well as
documentation for using dvd access with PC software
dvd players. Please read the instructions within the
documentation and follow accordingly.